TEACH YOUR TEEN TO DRIVE
... AND STAY ALIVE

Guidebook for Parents
Eight simple lifesaving lessons

Currently, 46 states and Washington, DC, require parents to teach their teens to drive for an average of 50 hours (in addition to any mandated formal driver education and training). This little book helps your teen to meet these requirements with positive, safe driving techniques that will last a lifetime.

Published 2012 by Traffic Safety Consultants, Inc.

Teach Your Teen to Drive... and stay alive:
A *guidebook for parents in eight simple lessons*

by Brett Elkins and Bruce Elkins

Printed in the United States of America

Disclaimer

Please read closely before proceeding.

Traffic Safety Consultants, Inc. (TSC), publishes this book on the condition that its readers and users acknowledge and agree that driving a car carries risks and that TSC, the book's authors, TSC employees and associates, book resellers or others responsible for making this book available—collectively in this disclaimer hereinafter referred to as 'We'—provide this book solely as information. By providing the book 'We' do not offer to readers and users any type of professional, legal, parental, psychological or other advice. The contents represent the sole opinions, discretions, and expressions of the authors; 'We' offer no warranties or guarantees, actual or implied, for the contents of the book. 'We' shall not be liable for emotional, financial, personal, physical, psychological, business, or other damages—including commercial, incidental, or consequential—that occur from driving a car or that occur in any connection to reading or using this book. The publisher and authors intend this book for reading and use by parents and teens who have passed the driving test of their state and who have taken a professional driver education and training course, where required—and which the authors highly recommend. 'We' make this book available solely to assist you, not to make driving or safety decisions for you. Please consult your state's laws for the final authority on traffic rules and driving requirements.

Baseball is like driving,
it's the one who gets home safely that counts.
— Tommy Lasorda

CONGRATULATIONS!

You have chosen a unique program that can save your teen's life and be an adventure of a lifetime without ever having to leave your own community. Teaching your teen to drive takes time, dedication, and responsibility, but your efforts will most certainly enable your son or daughter to become a much safer, aware, and cautious driver.

The fact that you are reading this guidebook indicates you are taking this responsibility seriously. Be proud that you are truly a special and concerned parent (or guardian) who cares about the safety and well-being of your teenager. This course helps to cover the requirements in all 50 states for parent-teen education of up to 50 hours.[1]

As we know, teenage years are a time of change. Adolescents often feel a need to break free from their parents, to establish independence and discover themselves. Driving is often the beginning of a teenager's transition to adulthood, and your guidance will pay long-term dividends.

This course is designed to provide continuing education thru proven defensive driving techniques. Together, using eight simple step-by-step lessons, we apply our unique success system:

The *Teach Your Teen* Fabulous, Amazing Success System

Ice Cream Drill => Bonding => Improved Performance => **Success!**

In this driving guidebook—written especially for parents and guardians who provide follow-on driver training for their teen—we have incorporated several special features that will be useful along the way. Please refer to the section 'Using this Guidebook' for details.

---

[1] Note: every state has different requirements so please consult your state new-driver rules for these specifics. The specific parent-teen requirements are found at: www.ghsa.org/html/stateinfo/laws/license_laws.html

Table of Contents

Acknowledgements
How a Tragedy Made this Book a Reality

This book was written over several years taking many interesting twists and turns along the way. The project was ultimately completed as a tribute to Joyce Kirsch, a loving neighbor who was tragically killed in a collision.

We initiated the book because we knew that by effectively incorporating humor and traffic safety into teen driving we could someday save many readers' lives. We felt that by empowering parents and teens with interesting facts, figures, stories, and our passion for safety, you, our fun-loving readers, would have the tools and decision-making skills needed to avoid collisions before they happen.

As a blanket gesture, let me thank and acknowledge everyone who has meant so much to me in my journey of life—a journey increasingly devoted to 'bringing 'em back alive.' For the book, specifically: thank you to my father and coauthor Bruce Elkins, one of the country's preeminent authorities on traffic safety; to our incredible, hardworking staff at Traffic Safety Consultants, Inc., particularly Rick Ehlers and Lawrence Gentilluci; and to editor Brian R. Wright.

The book also is dedicated as a tribute to our beloved founder Harlean Elkins and to our family: my loving wife Deborah, children Dane, Jaden, Cody, and Madison Elkins; and Dr. Brad, his wife Staci, and children Ryan, Kyle, and Cassy Elkins.

Brett Elkins
January 6, 2012
Panorama City, California

Using This Guidebook

Throughout the course, you will notice some life changing features illustrating points we believe can make a difference. Look for the following special notices with their corresponding icons:

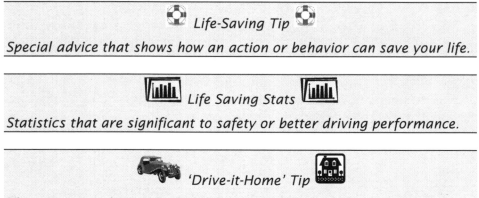

⊕ *Life-Saving Tip* ⊕

Special advice that shows how an action or behavior can save your life.

📊 *Life Saving Stats* 📊

Statistics that are significant to safety or better driving performance.

🚗 *'Drive-it-Home' Tip* 🏠

These are tips that make sense for your safety and your pocketbook.

We feel these special notices are important because our goal in writing this guidebook is to provide your teen with the necessary tools to possibly save their[2] life (and for that matter your life) by making you both safer and more aware drivers.

This guidebook has a unique design: Anyone, whether you drive professionally for a living or you're a mother unfamiliar with general vehicle parts and maintenance, can effectively teach traffic safety information logically and methodically to their teen (child or person for whom the adult driver is responsible). Go at your teen's pace, just a few hours a week. And don't be surprised, parent, if teaching your teen to drive makes *you* a better driver, too! ☺

The guidebook has been divided into two convenient sections: Part 1 contains general driving information important for you, the parent, to know especially before actually driving with your teen. Part 2 contains the actual, behind-the-wheel lessons and drills that enhance your teen's driving abilities. (We also publish an addendum, *Teach Your Teen, Plus,* which contains reference information—mainly other lessons and drills,

---

[2] In this guidebook, we adopt the convention of using (as a 'nonsexist' singular pronoun): 'they' for 'he or she' and 'them' for 'him or her' and 'their' for 'his or her.'

forms, background information—to download as a portable domain format (pdf) file for no charge at www.TeenDrivingOnline.com.)

Starting with the first lesson, we will help prepare you, the parent, for your new role as your teen's 'Coach.' That's right, instead of thinking of 'teaching your teen to drive,' think of yourself as *coaching* them to be the best driver possible. Like any good coach, you will try and bring out the best in your teen by encouraging them and supporting them. Like any good coach you will recommend practice, practice, and more practice. If you were coaching anyone, would you tell them that there would be only one practice each month?

So, Coach, get ready to *practice.*

 NOTE:

What you do in the next few weeks may save the life of someone you love.

In each lesson, we have a novel approach in which each drill is performed three times by the parent, then three times by the teen, which:

1) enables your teen to simply watch you first with what is expected without becoming nervous or frightened.

2) lets you the parent or guardian emphasize what is expected.

3) provides multiple completions of the same important principle: repetition leads to rapid gain of confidence behind the wheel.

During each lesson, consider what was learned in the previous lesson. Have your teen repeat each lesson until you are absolutely confident they are capable of that step. We are building the skills necessary to succeed, not worrying about how many times a lesson is performed. Some lessons, such as night driving or 'conquering' freeway driving, demand more practice than others. Remember the old joke:

> *Like any good coach, you will try and bring out the best in your teen by encouraging them and supporting them. Like any good coach you will recommend practice, practice and more practice.*

How do you get to Carnegie Hall?
Practice, practice, practice.

In many states, teenagers, legally must complete up to 50 hours of behind-the-

---

wheel, parental-supervised training. The parent or guardian then certifies to the state that this behind-the-wheel training has been completed in order to obtain a regular driver's license.

This guidebook contains 25-50 hours of lessons and drills. But even if you finish the course in, say, 30 hours, relax. Let your teen be the family's 'designated driver' for the additional 20 hours. Or you may find a teen requires *more* than 50 hours. Additional useful guidance material is located in the online addendum, *Teach Your Teen, Plus*, at www.TeenDrivingOnline.com.

NOTE:

Even if your teen has taken a formal driver education course, our guidebook is a valuable tool in assisting you in the development of your teen's driving ability.

Important Information Icons and Notes

Important or useful or urgent information that you should be aware of is indicated with the following icons:

NOTE

Essential but non-critical information. These messages should be read carefully as any directions or instructions contained therein can help you avoid mistakes.

IMPORTANT!

'Important' messages appear where the information may save you from critical or expensive conditions, either through driving or through behavior and equipment related to driving.

CAUTION!

Precautionary messages help you reduce the chance of injury or accident and avoid problems in the driving environment.

Traffic Safety Consultants, Inc.

 **WARNING!**

Warnings appear where overlooked details may cause serious problems that would not otherwise be attended to.

 **TIP or IDEA**

These messages inform the reader of relevant facts that may apply to your situation. Knowing these may save you trouble, or simply make your day more stress free.

 DEFINITION

Either a definition or 'what's that word?' or a question to illustrate a point.

LIGHTER TURN

Contains a quotation or humorous observation, e.g.
"When buying a used vehicle, punch the buttons on the radio. If all the stations are rock and roll, there's a good chance the transmission is shot!" — Larry Lujack

 **ICE CREAM DRILL**

What we've concocted as a reward to follow the so-called 'Culmination Drill'—in which the teen performs all lesson drills in a single session. The Ice Cream Drill is for celebrating and bonding by enjoying together ice cream or yogurt, coffee, dinner or desert. It is most readers' favorite drill. ☺

1: Driver Education

It's Serious Business Out Here

Part 1 is the essential information that you and your teen will need before getting behind the wheel of a '3000 pound loaded weapon.' But not to worry, we shall arm you with a wealth of fun facts, figures, and "how to's" to make your job easy and effective.

Look forward to this opportunity to 'teach your teen' all you know, and perhaps even help to save your teen's life—through the performance and safety information herein. Relax and enjoy the natural process of being a 'coach,' once again, in this essential part of the all-American game of life. The memories will remain with you always.

The buzz: Important subjects in this section are:

- ☐ A mom's letter to her son
- ☐ The teen dilemma
- ☐ The subliminal message
- ☐ A parent's quiz
- ☐ Parental rights
- ☐ Who's *seeing* what
- ☐ Parent/teen driving contract

First, let's look at the downside of driving, what can happen if the lessons are not learned, or you make a big mistake. Teen, we focus on *success* in this booklet; always picture in your mind you're driving competently, skillfully, even enjoyably. But *know* the grim alternative.

❂ Life-Saving Tip ❂

The following letter was written by a mother to her son following his death in a vehicle crash—caused by mixing driving with drugs. Please take a moment to read this special letter with your son or daughter. Afterward, ask your teen what the son, or mother, might have done differently to have kept him alive.

Letter to a Lost Son

May you never have to write a letter like this:

Dear David,

How are you? We are not fine. Wish you were here. Last Friday, I had a funny thing happen to me. I went into the candy store to buy some chocolate Easter eggs, and then realized I had to buy three instead of four. Right there in the store, the tears started streaming down my face, just like someone opened up a faucet. The clerk asked me if I was having an allergy attack. I guess I was. I'm allergic to death.

Thursday, after the funeral, Dad called up the guy who hit you. Poor man, how he is suffering. Dad told him it's okay. We know there was nothing he could have done to prevent it. You were going 70 and ran the red light. First, I thought it was the Ludes that made you drive like a maniac, but Tami told me you always drove like you were on the Indianapolis Speedway. She was always telling you to slow down and stop for lights.

Kenny told me, because you loved cars, driving was a challenge. How to get to the next place in the fastest possible time. Weaving in and out of lanes, always speeding.

David, one day last week we were driving to the cemetery and a guy in a van ran the red on Topanga. I wish we could have caught up with him and introduced him to his future, if he didn't change his way of driving. Kids your age all think accidents, like cancer, happen to someone else. No way! You can't beat the system. Sooner or later the statistics catch up with you.

I'm sorry you're never going to make that million dollars you always talked about, but more sorry you couldn't get help with all your problems and took out your frustrations behind the wheel. By the way, I'm also relieved there is now no chance of you hitting some little, innocent five-year-old on his bike. I couldn't have handled that.

We all loved you, but were completely helpless. You had to do everything your way. Well, say hello to God for me. I hope you're at peace now. We're not.

Love,

Mom

The Teen Dilemma

The following list shows important statistics on the dangers of teen driving... due to teens' inexperience and general overconfidence. Please read the list twice and discuss with your teen the steps they can take to reduce their chances of ending up as one of these statistics.

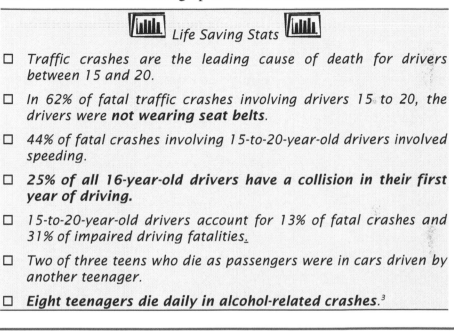

Life Saving Stats

☐ *Traffic crashes are the leading cause of death for drivers between 15 and 20.*

☐ *In 62% of fatal traffic crashes involving drivers 15 to 20, the drivers were **not wearing seat belts**.*

☐ *44% of fatal crashes involving 15-to-20-year-old drivers involved speeding.*

☐ ***25% of all 16-year-old drivers have a collision in their first year of driving.***

☐ *15-to-20-year-old drivers account for 13% of fatal crashes and 31% of impaired driving fatalities.*

☐ *Two of three teens who die as passengers were in cars driven by another teenager.*

☐ ***Eight teenagers die daily in alcohol-related crashes.***[3]

🪀 IMPORTANT!

A car is a 3000-pound loaded weapon. To help you stay alive and thrive, the authors will never sugarcoat safety.

Please, both of you take your driving responsibilities *very seriously*, ensuring each lesson is mastered. In general, as the above stats point out, we do a poor job in this country learning to drive safely. Still, together—with patience, practice, and persistence—we can make a fundamental difference in your teen's driving ability.

Ready?!

---

[3] Sources: NHTSA, 2007 Crash Facts, Young Drivers MADD, www.madd.org

Subliminal Message

Parent, you may not realize it, but you started teaching your youngling to drive many years ago. Driving lessons started when you first drove with your baby in the backseat. Your driving habits have been carefully observed ever since that moment and it is likely your teen has acquired many of your driving tendencies... the good *and* the bad.

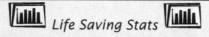 *Life Saving Stats*

From a recent transportation study of teenagers:

- 🌐 *40% have witnessed their parents swearing at other drivers.*
- 🌐 *20% claim their parents often make rude gestures while driving.*
- 🌐 *30% say their parents honk the horn and flash lights in anger.*

Also from the study, most teenagers say they tend to emulate the driving habits of their father.

Some of the messages are subliminal. Like the father who tailgates. The child never mentions this fact to their dad, and Dad of course does not say, "Hey, son, have you noticed I tailgate?" The subliminal message, however, is that tailgating is not dangerous, because Dad never would do anything to harm me (or anyone else); he loves me.

Same for speeding. For more than ten years, children have observed  their parents and other adults speed—often with the suggestion "Don't worry, police won't ticket you unless you're 10 mph over." So, when the child starts to drive, guess what speed they travel? Yep, 10 over.

 NOTE

Most experienced drivers will tell you that posted speed limits are generally reasonable.

Lessons learned early are hard to break

Are you a calm driver? Courteous? Cautious? Do you drive defensively? Then your teen will be and do likewise. But what if you are an angry driver? Impatient? Aggressive... a speed-o-holic? Are you distracted by your cellphone? Your lunch? Your mascara? Do you fail to check your mirrors before turning? Then don't be surprised when your teen reaches into the backseat for a CD on the freeway at 65 mph.

A Special Word about Distractions

The table below shows a recent list from the California Highway Patrol of the most dangerous distractions.

Table 1: Numbers of Collisions per Distraction

Distraction	No.
Cell phones	913
Radio or CD	769
Children	328
Eating/drinking	259
Reading	168
Smoking	115
Electronics (Computer, fax, etc)	81
Animals	76
Personal grooming	28
Other	5,227

Clearly the distraction *du jour* in America—and probably many other countries—is the cellular phone, especially the so-called smartphone that enables a user to manually key in text messages. Most states have laws against texting and driving.

Studies have shown that drivers are four times more likely to have a collision while merely talking on a cellphone. Texting is much worse. Practically, you should avoid cell chat while driving... and

ABSOLUTELY, YOU MUST NEVER TEXT WHILE DRIVING.

First Things First

Okay, parent, you know how to drive... but how about the traffic laws?

Before your teen received a learner's permit, he/she had to pass a test at your state's motor vehicle agency. When was the last time you tested *your* knowledge of the traffic laws? You can avoid being embarrassed by picking up a copy of the 'Rules of the Road' pamphlet at your local motor vehicle or highway safety office.

Parent, complete this simple quiz to determine your knowledge of the rules of the road. Pass = 7 out of 10. Repeat as needed.

Table 2: Quiz for Parent or Guardian

#	Question	True	False
1	In some circumstances, you may receive a traffic citation for going through a green traffic signal.		
2	It is legal to drive barefooted.		
3	The first driver at a four-way-stop intersection always has the right of way.		
4	A driver may travel faster than the posted (or listed) speed limit in order to pass another vehicle.		
5	The legal definition of driving impaired, for an adult, is operating a motor vehicle with a blood alcohol content (BAC) of 0.08 or above.		
6	If no speed limits are posted, you can go as fast as you wish.		
7	You may cross a double-yellow center line if the car ahead of you is traveling below the posted speed limit.		
8	Law enforcement officers must permit drivers to travel up to 10 mph over the posted speed limit before stopping them for speeding.		
9	If no traffic exists at an intersection, a driver does not have to come to a complete stop at a stop sign.		
10	It is legal to pull into an intersection on a green light and stop in the intersection to make a left turn and wait until the traffic from the opposite direction stops before making the left turn.		

Answers:

1. **True.** The law requires drivers to use 'due care' to avoid a collision. If an officer can prove in court that you were operating your vehicle in an unsafe manner when you went through a green light, you can receive a traffic citation.

2. **True.** In most states it is not against the law to drive barefooted. However, it is never a good practice to drive bare footed or even with flip-flops. Why? You need foot support and proper gripping to accurately engage the gas and the brakes. Bare feet and flip-flops are dangerous for driving.

3. **False.** State laws never give the right of way to one party over another. The law states who has the right of way under what circumstances. But this does not entitle a driver to crash into another driver by arguing he had the right of way.

4. **False.** It is never legal to travel above the posted speed limit, unless you are driving an authorized emergency vehicle with the emergency lights and siren activated.

5. **True.** For all states legal definition of impairment is now 0.08 BAC. However, in many states even half a drink for a teen can result in an automatic DUI.

6. **False**. Every state has a set speed limit.

7. **False**. You may never legally cross a double-yellow line.

8. **False.** One mph over the speed limit is a violation of the posted speed limit law. Officers do not legally have to allow for any deviation.

9. **False**. No provision in any state law permits drivers to run a legally posted stop sign, even if no other traffic is present.

10. **True (or False)** depending upon the state. This action varies from state to state. It most states it is legal; but it is not a safe practice. If you are aware ahead of time that an intersection always has heavy traffic from the opposite direction, consider going straight then around the block making right turns until you are able to travel straight through the intersection.

How did you do? Please review your test results with your teen to show them that even parents have room to improve.

Teenager + Parent = The 'Perfect Driver'

Young people are often in better shape. Their vision, hearing and reflexes are sharp; they are alert and agile. Physically speaking, younger drivers have the potential to be the best drivers on the road. But teenagers lack experience, maturity, and, often, good judgment... which peer pressure can impair. Parents have experience and, hopefully, good judgment.

If we as parents could combine the physical attributes of our children with our own good sense and judgment born of hundreds of thousands of miles behind the wheel of a motor vehicle, that would represent the 'perfect driver.' This is the formula by which you, the parent, can successfully *coach* your teen to drive and stay alive!

Finally, mom or dad, you have the ultimate bargaining chip:

 **SPECIAL BARGAINING CHIP**

In most states, no one under the age of 18 may obtain a
learner's permit or a driver license without parental consent.

Use this bargaining chip wisely. Just because your teen is begging you for permission to start learning to drive doesn't mean that they are ready. Here's a checklist to help you judge.

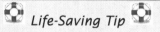 *Life-Saving Tip*

Does your teen have these qualities? Check each box that applies!

( ) Takes on responsibilities.
( ) Is very dedicated.
( ) Is well organized.
( ) Is a good student.
( ) **Makes good decisions [big life saver].**
( ) Has an excellent memory.
( ) Is punctual.
( ) Enjoys reading.
( ) Emotionally mature/stable.
( ) Enjoys sports or other hobbies.
( ) Has a musical background/plays instruments.
( ) Helps with chores.

The more boxes you check, the greater your teen's readiness. If your teen is not ready you must be prepared to make a difficult decision and delay their permit or license.

Further, a parent has the right to have their teen driver's license *revoked* any time before their 18th birthday. So, if they do not obey your rules and curfews, keep their room clean, or later if they fail to work hard in school and earn decent grades, you can revoke their driving privilege.

Importance of Good Vision

Before beginning the actual driving lessons outlined in this guidebook, we highly recommend taking your teenager to an optometrist or an ophthalmologist for an eye exam. If your teen cannot see clearly, collisions are more likely.

Also, a teen's vision changes frequently, sometimes every few months. So check their vision annually during these formative years.

... we highly recommend taking your teenager to an optometrist or an ophthalmologist for an eye exam.

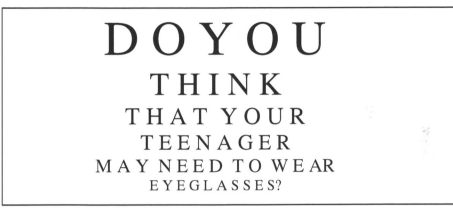

D O Y O U
T H I N K
T H A T   Y O U R
T E E N A G E R
M A Y   N E E D   T O   W E A R
E Y E G L A S S E S ?

The Driving Contract

What is the Parent-Teen Driving Contract?

A parent-teen driving contract is a formal agreement between parent(s) and their teen driver that outlines specific guidelines that parents and teens agree to follow. It also establishes consequences and discussion for not following the agreement.

Parents and their teen should discuss the driving contract and enter into the contract as partners. Each party should dedicate enough time to thoroughly read and discuss all the parts of the contract before beginning any behind-the-wheel lessons. The next page shows a single-page sample contract (the 8.5" x 11" version may be accessed in our *Teach Your Teen, Plus* addendum at www.TeenDrivingOnline.com.) Use as a template for your own.

PARENT-TEEN DRIVING CONTRACT

Teen Commitment:

A.   I will not drive between 11:00 p.m. and 5:00 a.m. (the most dangerous time period to operate a motor vehicle). This rule will remain in place for the first 12 months from the date I get my driver license.

B.   I will obey the posted speed limit and adjust my vehicle's speed according to weather and road conditions. I will not drive when angry, frustrated, or emotional. I will not tailgate, speed, weave in and out of traffic, or participate in any aggressive or reckless driving behavior.

C.   I will never consume alcohol or use drugs and then drive. I agree that I will never ride in a vehicle with someone who has consumed any amount of alcohol or has been using drugs. I will call you if I am ever in a situation I feel unsafe for me to drive or unsafe for me to ride with someone else, and I will take alternative transportation in those conditions.

D.   I will wear my safety belt at all times. I will not ride in a vehicle as a passenger without wearing the vehicle's seat belt. I will not ride in a vehicle if the driver and other passengers are not properly restrained.

E.   I will not have any passengers in the vehicle during my first year of driving unless you or someone you have approved in advance is present. I will not be a passenger in any vehicle where I do not feel comfortable or safe.

F.   I agree that, while driving, I will not use a wireless telephone, pager, laptop computer, or any other electronic communications or mobile services device to speak or text in any manner, even 'handsfree.' I agree to keep all such electronic gear stored safely, secured in the locked trunk or glove compartment.

G.   I will not look away from the road or be distracted from driving. If I am not able to focus on the driving task due to lack of sleep or if I am emotional, I will not drive. I will not allow passengers to distract me.

I understand these rules are for my safety. If I violate any of these rules, I agree to lose my driving privileges for _____ *(time period).*

Additional penalties (if any): _____

Parent Commitment:

Your safety is my number one priority and I will be there when you need me. I will come and get you wherever you are, whatever the time of day or night if you are not able to get home because you are following our rules or are abiding by any state laws and do not feel comfortable driving or being a passenger in a vehicle.

I promise not to become angry and will rationally discuss at a later time your reasons for asking for assistance. I also promise to lead by example, always being properly restrained, not talking or texting on a cell phone while driving, and obeying the traffic laws of our state. I promise not to raise my voice with you while you are driving and to make productive and positive suggestions. I promise to continually improve my driving skills, just as you are improving your driving skills.

Signatures:

Teen   _____   Date _____/_____/_____
        Signature

Parent(s) _____   Date _____/_____/_____
        Signatures

        _____

Parent Safety Tips

The following guidelines will help you set important and potentially life changing rules for your teenage driver. And teenagers, as you know, need boundaries. Be fair... but be firm. Let you teen know that any failure to abide by your driving policies outlined above in the teen contract will result in their driving privileges being suspended.

❑ First, remember as a parent you are a role model. When you speed (even only 10 mph over the limit), run red or yellow lights, tailgate, and/or commit other violations, that's a poor example for your teen.

❑ Give your new teen driver as much experience as possible before they drive on their own.

❑ Set strict guidelines about the use of seat belts for the driver and all passengers. Most accidents occur within a few miles of your home, so buckle up.

❑ Discuss and write down the consequences for any incidents of drug and alcohol use. (Ref. parent-teen contract.)

❑ Restrict the number of passengers. A good rule is to have no more than one nonfamily member in the vehicle while the teen is driving. Each additional driver increases distraction and risk of a collision. Like clever vanity plates... ☺

❑ Limit night driving. A study in Europe shows more than 40% of accidents occur at night, even if the number of drivers at night are far fewer than during the day.

❑ Ensure your teen driver gets practice—with an experienced, legally licensed driver in the vehicle—in hazardous weather conditions.

❑ Do not use cellular telephones, even hands-free systems, while driving a motor vehicle.

❑ Choose a safe vehicle. Sports vehicles and small vehicles are not the best options for 'bringing them back alive.'

❑ Consider having your teen pay for the additional cost of vehicle insurance.

⛒ *Life-Saving Tip* ⛒

Is your car safe enough to let your teen drive in it? Make sure by checking 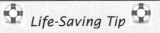 (a government crash test safety site).

 **IMPORTANT!**

It matters little how well a teen can play a sport, excel in school, or do anything in life if they lose that life in a traffic crash.

So, you're still anxious about your teen driving?

It's only natural. You have doubts about being 'the Coach' and doubts about your teen's ability to learn. Well, consider that your teen is probably involved in some kind of sport: soccer, baseball, skateboarding, golf, tennis, rollerblading, and so on. Or perhaps your teen plays a musical instrument. They get better and better with time.

Learning to drive is similar to playing a sport or a musical instrument. And at the outset of the learning process, each individual movement is made separately and with conscious deliberation. The brain for a short time becomes overloaded in mastering these simple movements. But with enough repetition, the tasks eventually feel natural and can be accomplished without actually 'thinking about it.'

Common Characteristics of Lessons and Drills

These are the common characteristics of the drills:

> *Learning to drive is similar to playing a sport or a musical instrument.*

1. Read the entire lesson. Be mentally prepared! Relax and have fun.

2. Discuss the lesson with your teen so they'll know what to expect.

3. Perform each drill three times *first*, then your teen takes the wheel.

4. Teen performs each drill three times to learn through repetition.

5. Culmination Drill: the teen performs all drills in a single session.

6. 'Ice Cream Drill:' This step is important as the single experience and memory that you and your child will never forget going out together to get ice cream, yogurt, a smoothie, coffee, dinner, dessert, etc.

REMEMBER:

This is a FLEXIBLE plan. You may want to devote more than one session to each lesson—especially in the intermediate and advanced levels. No session should last longer than one hour.

It will be a breeze...

But a few things to remember first:

The three most important qualities of a good coach:

1. Patience
2. More patience
3. Even more patience

Stay calm... keeping the nerves at bay

Safe drivers are calm and relaxed. If you're nervous, you can expect your teen to be nervous, too. So be sure to stay calm, be gentle, and above all... expect mistakes. Mistakes are okay—it's how we learn, remember? Praise fully. NEVER, NEVER scream or yell at your teen. If you feel yourself getting anxious or upset, stop the lesson for that day.

The less talk the better

During the lessons—especially when your teen is behind the wheel—take special care not to talk *at* them. Keep your comments short and to the point: "Slow down." "Signal." "Brake." Too much talking distracts from performance. Lengthy discussions should take place with the vehicle parked and both parties at ease, no distractive noise.

Remember, since you will not make eye contact with your teen while the vehicle is in motion, the two of you may experience frustration over communications. When words fail, it's a good idea to have your teen pull to the side of the road. Then you can take the wheel yourself and demonstrate exactly what you mean.

Your teen is never 'right' (or left... alone) ☺

🛟 Life-Saving Tip 🛟

When answering your teen's questions during your driving sessions, always use the words **"yes"** or **"correct"** when answering in the affirmative. Hearing the word "right" may inadvertently compel them to suddenly swerve to the right or make an unwanted right turn.

Use 'surprise stops'

During the first few lessons, we recommend that you frequently and suddenly say, "Stop!" [Choose safe places and moments for this—alone on a quiet side street with no vehicles to the rear.] Surprise stops help to cultivate your teen's reaction ability.

The surprise stop also prepares your teen to react to hazards ahead that you see and they miss—such as a driver exiting a parked car or a bike rider heading into the street from the right sidewalk.

⚠ IMPORTANT!

For safety, we recommend that you place a mirror on the passenger side sun visor, so that you are able to see clearly to the rear before initiating the 'surprise stop' for your teen.

The Additional Teen Driving Hours Requirement

In most states, in addition to formal driver's training, parents or guardians are required to supervise their teen's driving for generally another 50 hours or so. A word to the wise: a 50-hour requirement is relatively easy to meet. Thus, we encourage you—after the first three lessons of the guidebook—to have your teen drive everywhere you feel it is comfortable and safe to do so. The extra parent-guided training will give them more confidence.

Driving Log

The table on the next page provides a convenient driving log for tracking progress in the lessons and drills. An 8.5 x 11 inch version of the driving log is available from the *Teach Your Teen, Plus* addendum at www.TeenDrivingOnline.com.

50-Hour Driving Log

Date Hrs.	Driving Skill Practiced	Comments	Adult Initials
_____			
_____			
_____			
_____			
_____			
_____			
_____			
_____			
_____			
_____			
_____			
_____			
_____			
_____			
_____			

2: DRIVER TRAINING

"DO AND YOU UNDERSTAND"—LESSONS AND DRILLS

Driving with your teen and practicing with them will be a memory that you will both cherish forever. Have fun on your journey. But remember, the point of these lessons and drills is to encourage your teen make the correct choices... leading to Option 1 as opposed to Option 2 below.

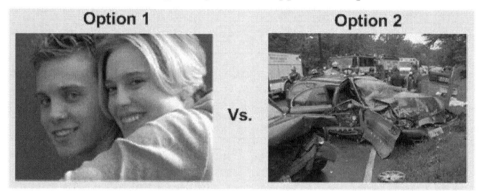

Your teens should hold the Option 1 image of life and happiness in their minds at all times. Yet to be aware of the grim consequences of failure (Option 2) can emphasize the importance of getting it right. Driving isn't difficult, but YOU NEED ALWAYS TO PAY ATTENTION.

We hope you are as excited as your teen to begin the first few lessons.

LESSON #1
The ABCs of Driver Training

TEEN STATISTIC

Car crashes are the leading cause of death for teenagers. According to the Center for Disease Control (CDC), every day nine teenagers die from car injuries. Speeding accounts for about a third of these deaths and alcohol a quarter. Our goal in writing this guidebook is to help your teen drive, thrive, and stay alive. Together we will make a difference.

Lesson #1 Summary

What We'll Cover	Using items in your car (e.g. head rest), starting and stopping drills, and going forward/backwards.

Location	A quiet, local parking lot that has more than one lane or route of travel, such as a church parking lot with no traffic.
Suggested Time	Saturday or Sunday morning around 8 a.m.
Speed Limits	0 TO 20 mph depending on the drill.
Parent Instruction	Drive to a local parking lot that you have selected in advance, which has more than one lane/area of travel. Repeat lesson if desired.

 NOTE

Make sure to take this moment and go over your car's owner's manual and show your teen how the index will help them locate almost any function of the car and even how to add oil.

Parent completes each drill three times first then the teen driver completes the drill three times.

Drill 1: CONTROLS AND EQUIPMENT ----------------------

Please drive to a quiet and safe location you have determined ahead of time. It is important that you always select a location in advance *before* the lesson starts. Park the vehicle at the location, engage the emergency brake, and shut off the engine, leaving down the windows for air.

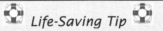 *Life-Saving Tip*

Every year approximately 50 people (and 1000s of animals) die when left in the car with the windows rolled up. Even at a normal outside temperature, a human, especially a young child, can die due to the large temperature increase in a closed vehicle with rolled up windows.

Seatbelts

Life-Saving Tip

*The single most important safety feature on your car is your seatbelt. Remind your teen that unless they 'click it,' they may end up with a ticket—hopefully not one up to heaven. Seatbelts save thousands of lives annually. Wearing a seatbelt is a prerequisite for driving. Statistics from the National Highway Traffic Safety Administration (NHTSA) show that approximately 6,000 young occupants die annually in car collisions and more than 4,000 are **not** wearing seat belts.*

Seat belts must be properly secured *before* the car starts; never during or after the drive begins. Many drivers and passengers are injured or killed while *sitting in a parked car* without a seatbelt when another car blindsides them. Seatbelts are without question the single most important factor in saving lives in a crash.

Statistically speaking, assume that you or your teen will be involved in a major accident in your lifetime. So it is best to prepare yourselves for this event now. Have your teen practice putting on and taking off their seatbelt... every time they enter the car. You, too. It's easy to fall into bad habits e.g. 'clickit in transit.' Do it right: clickit *before* transit. You know in your heart it's the right thing to do. — Coach

Remaining Controls and Equipment

In the interests of being concise, we refer the reader to the online addendum *Teach Your Teen, Plus* at www.TeenDrivingOnline.com for detailed comments and descriptions about the following important controls and equipment. Parent, go over each of these items in detail with your teen.

IMPORTANT!

Understanding details of how your car operates can save your life. For example, if it started hailing and your teen cannot locate or operate the windshield wiper, they are risking their life scrambling around in a panic trying to find it.

- ☐ Head Rests—need to be properly positioned, too high or too low can have fatal consequences.
- ☐ Rearview and Side Mirrors—ref. several drills in the addendum, *Teach Your Teen, Plus* (www.TeenDrivingOnline.com).
- ☐ Foot Brake—before learning to go, learn to stop.
- ☐ Gas Pedal—where to apply the go.
- ☐ Parking Brake or Emergency Brake—there's a difference.
- ☐ Steering Wheel—put the hands at 9 and 3 or 10 and 2 per hands of the clock; these are the safest hand positions.
- ☐ Ignition Components—key or keyless, that is the key ☺
- ☐ Seat Adjustment Controls—manual or auto, no slouching; the entire seat belt needs to harness you securely.
- ☐ Climate Control—always 'keep your cool'... by adjusting the controls *before* you drive.

☐ Windshield Wiper/Washer—no streaky streaky.

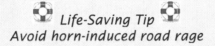

🛟 *Life-Saving Tip* 🛟

Your car manufacturer advocates changing windshield wiper blades once a year. When was the last time your wipers were changed?

☐ Light Switch—see the light.

☐ Turn Signal Indicators—tell others which way you're going.

☐ High Beam—not to blind others as you wish not to be blinded; only use when dark and no cars are near.

☐ Transmission—getting it in gear.

☐ Speedometer—"I have NO need for speed."

☐ Fuel Gauge—don't play chicken with an empty tank; you don't want to run out of gas in a dangerous neighborhood, and stalling out on a high speed thoroughfare can be life-threatening.

☐ Horn—like the Roadrunner, it's 'beep beep' except...

🛟 *Life-Saving Tip* 🛟
Avoid horn-induced road rage

Two quick beeps is the proper and courteous method. In a quiet area, have your teen give it a honk and have them practice the two quick beeps on their new instrument, the horn. Only 'lay on horn' in emergencies to get the attention of an unwary driver about to crash.

☐ Airbag(s)—just say NO to a false sense of security

🛟 *Life-Saving Tip* 🛟

Seatbelts must be worn in conjunction with airbags. NEVER rely on just the airbag. The driver should sit at least 12 inches away from the airbag. Do not deactivate this device.

☐ Hood Release—there's an engine in there, can you get at it?

☐ Gas Tank Cover Release—learn how to 'save your gass' ☺

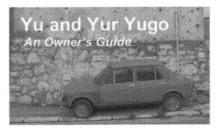

Parent and teen should both consult the online addendum, *as well as the car's owner's manual* for full descriptions of the above controls and equipment.

NOTE:

Take this moment to review your car's manual to look up how to add oil to your car and what kind of oil you should buy. All items are listed in the car's manual, which is a 'bible of information' that you want readily available. Always pull off the road in a safe place to review.

LIGHTER TURN

Two car radio antennas met in a parking lot, fell in love, and got married. The ceremony wasn't much, but the reception was excellent. — (ow, that one hurts. — Ed.)

DRILL 2: MIRROR USE ---

A drill to help your teen identify any blind spots in the mirrors

With the car shut off, the windows rolled down, and the emergency brake on for safety, parent: sit in the driver's seat and adjust the car's mirrors so they work best for you. Viewing the passenger's side mirror, ask your teen to exit the car and slowly walk to the back of the car to any point where you cannot see them. These are referred to as 'blind spots' and can be deadly if you don't notice a vehicle in one. Now, do the same drill using the rear view mirror instead. Have your teen walk behind your car until they reach a point that you cannot see them.

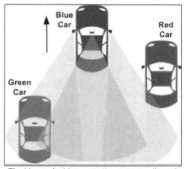

The blue car's driver sees the green car through his mirrors but cannot see the red car without turning to check his **blind spot**.

Now, it's your teen's turn to look for blind spots in both mirrors. Parent: have your teen switch to the driver's seat and adjust the car's mirrors so they work best for your teen. You the parent should exit the car and slowly move to the passenger side of the car until you enter the blind spot. Please walk slowly behind your car to a spot where your teen cannot see you in the driver's side rearview mirror and then the center rearview mirror. When finished, the parent should get back into the car and explain that the areas where they could not be seen are called blind spots or 'no zones.'

DRILL 3: GAS-BRAKE DRILL---------------------------------

Conduct this drill three times, then have your teen conduct the drill.

Parent: while sitting in the driver's seat, both you and your teen will engage your seat belts. Your seats both should never recline too far back—so remind your teen that drivers should sit erect and alert—comfortable, but not so you slouch.

☸ *Life-Saving Tip* ☸

It is extremely dangerous for a passenger to sleep in a car in a reclining position. This can result in death during a collision as the reclining passenger may slip through the safety belt harness. Sleep straight up!

While the car is parked with the ignition/car switch off, parent, press the car's brake several times and let off the brake. Now, push on the accelerator or gas pedal several times. Finally, switch back and forth casually from the gas pedal to the brake pedal.

Now ask your teen to pretend they are a drill sergeant and call out in rapid succession the words: "Gas" or "Brake" in any order and you respond appropriately by pressing the gas pedal or brake pedal while the car is off. "Gas, gas, brake, gas, brake." Exit the car carefully and repeat the same drills by having your teen get into the driver seat while you become the drill sergeant… or 'Coach.' ☺

DRILL 4: BEGINNING DRIVING DRILLS --------------------

Drill #4 consists of six easy and fun beginning driving exercises.

Exercise 1: Driving Forward "Now you're making progress!"☺

The following drills will probably remind you of the time when you first taught your son or daughter to ride a bike. At this time, we recommend you take a picture of your teen driving and completing their first lesson of our course. We know it will be a treasured moment and please put it on Facebook with the caption: 'Teach Your Teen to Drive and Stay Alive… while mom or dad is a nervous wreck.'

📝 GENERAL PROCEDURE:

Conduct the exercises of this drill three times, then have your teen conduct the exercise three times. Choose a vacant parking lot with no cars or pedestrians present.

Proceed as follows:

1) While the car is parked, parent start the engine. Next, release the parking/emergency brake. Before driving forward (5-7 mph), place your right foot on the brake pedal so the car does not move at this point. Now, use or engage the car's gear shift level to the drive position ('D') so the car is able to move forward.

2) You will drive forward to a safe point that you select maybe 20-50 feet ahead and then slowly stop the car using your brakes. Put the vehicle in park position. Repeat this drill three times so they see how you are doing it. Then your teen does the drill three times.

Exercise 2: Driving Backward

Parent: before putting the car in reverse, make sure your right foot is firmly on the brake. Now, you will move backward (5-7 mph) by placing the gear lever into reverse (R). Look back over your right shoulder and slowly drive backward to a safe point you have selected maybe 20-50 feet ahead. Stop the vehicle and put it into park.

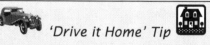

'Drive it Home' Tip

Never back up faster than a human being can walk. The average human foot-speed is 2-3 mph. So, it's quite possible to get a speeding ticket in reverse! ☺

Exercise 3: Driving Forward, ZigZag ...   ☺ no, not this kind→

Drive forward *slowly* in a zigzag pattern. While driving forward, for this drill, you will slowly turn the wheel slightly to the right for a short distance and then change the direction by steering your car to the left. Continue to repeat the pattern as long as you have room.

Exercise 4: Driving Forward, Making Figure 8s—go figure! ☺

Drive the car forward and circle around in a Figure 8 type of pattern to get used to controlling the car, slowing it, and steering it. This drill requires some mastery of movement so if your teen passes, it is a sign of future success.

Exercise 5: Driving Forward at 10 mph, Then Stopping

First drive forward at a speed approaching 10-15 mph. While you are driving, have your teen softly call out for you to "stop" and you will calmly press the brakes. This is our famous 'Surprise Stop' that you may want to complete in every lesson.

Exercise 6: Sudden Turn Going Forward

Drive forward (at a slow speed) and quickly turn the car to the right. Now continue to drive forward and turn the car to the left and repeat the drill going in the other direction.

For all exercises, switch positions and have your teen do them, too. Remind them of each drill before they do it. Be positive and relaxed.

CULMINATION DRILL ---

Once your teen has completed every drill above *three times* to your satisfaction, it's time for the so-called 'culmination drill,' in which your teen performs all of the drills together as a 'showcase performance.' Then they have truly mastered the lesson and it's time for the Ice Cream Drill. "How sweet is that!"

 ICE CREAM DRILL

Congratulations...you were both outstanding and now it's off to ice cream or yogurt, coffee, dinner or desert. You both earned it so go ahead and savor the moment. Most drivers find this drill their favorite. ☺

LIGHTER TURN

"When buying a used vehicle, punch the buttons on the radio. If all the stations are rock and roll, there's a good chance the transmission is shot!" — Larry Lujack

Don't Be Intimidated

You don't have to be an automobile mechanic to teach someone to drive. Think about this: your teen probably has a computer and spends time on the Internet. Well, driving a vehicle is like using a computer—you only need to learn operating techniques and procedures—you don't have to understand processor chips and motherboards. Same with cars, you can be a competent motorist without knowing how to fix a tranny.

TO CONSIDER... AFTER THIS COURSE

Many drivers of performance cars join groups of 'enthusiasts' who hold weekend 'performance and safety' driving events where drivers of all experience and skill levels learn to improve their driving technique on closed tracks. (Ref. High Performance Drivers Education on Wikipedia.) Most events allow, even encourage, non-performance car drivers to take part. Check out events in your area; they can significantly enhance your driving ability and confidence. (And they are FUN, FUN, FUN.) ☺

 I finally got some good news from my mechanic. He said my glove compartment and my sun visor are in great shape.

LESSON #2
Mastering Turns and Intersections

TEEN STATISTIC

According to the Federal Highway Administration, in 2008, 37,261 fatalities occurred on US roads. Of these, 7,772 (20.8%) were at intersections. Inexperience is a major factor: 16-year-olds have higher crash rates (w/three times the fatalities) than drivers of any other age.

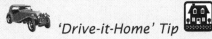

'Drive-it-Home' Tip

In 2011, State Farm Insurance found that approximately 20% of all drivers accessed a smart phone while driving. 'Drive it Home' now with a discussion of the dangers of accessing your cell phone while driving.

Lesson #2 Summary

What We'll Cover	Right turns, left turns, U-turns
Location	Local quiet residential streets and rural roadways.
Suggested Time	A weekend ~10 a.m.-11 a.m.. 45 to 60 minutes. Repeat lesson if desired.
Speed Limits	Up to 35 mph
Parent Instruction	Drive to the area you have chosen in advance. Hopefully you have planned a travel route in advance where the teen can operate the car at speeds between 25 to 35 mph. Parent completes all the drills once each in sequence. Teen performs all the drills once each in sequence, three times. [that is: 1, 2, 3, 4; 1, 2, 3, 4; 1, 2, 3, 4.]

Question: Why are turns more dangerous than straight ahead driving?

Answer: When turning, the driver faces additional challenges such as a car coming toward him or her plus pedestrian crossings, traffic lights, and traffic signs. Plus, you as the driver must be even more aware about changes in speed.

Question: What can happen to your car if you are speeding while attempting a turn?

Answer: Any car that makes a sudden turn at higher speed can literally flip and roll, resulting in serious injury or death.

DRILL 1: RIGHT TURN --

1) Parent: begin driving on the street. When about 100 feet from making a right turn, activate the right turn signal. (The drill assumes traffic is clear and you have the right of way.)

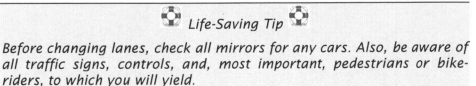

Life-Saving Tip

Before changing lanes, check all mirrors for any cars. Also, be aware of all traffic signs, controls, and, most important, pedestrians or bike-riders, to which you will yield.

2) Place both hands on the wheel and make a smooth right turn into the right lane of the intersecting roadway. Allow the wheel to return to the fingers. Proceed directly to Drill 2.

 **REMEMBER**

Right turns are usually preceded by a lane change in which the vehicle is moved safely into the curb lane.

DRILL 2: LEFT TURN (AND THEN IT WILL BE U-TURN ☺)

Proceed as follows:

1) Parent: Continue driving on the street and approximately 100 feet before making a left turn, please activate your left turn indicator. Before changing lanes, be sure to check all mirrors for any cars. Be aware of all traffic signs, controls, and, most important, pedestrians or bike-riders.

2) Before making a left turn always look 'Left-Right-Left.'[4] Both hands are on the steering wheel. When traffic is clear, accelerate and turn the wheel to the left. Make a smooth left turn into an available lane of the intersecting roadway. Allow the steering wheel to return to the fingers. Stop and return to Drill 1.

Three rights = one left. As a general rule, making a right turn is safer than a left. If you want to avoid left turns, you can use this formula to navigate the neighborhood. The trick is to drive only one block past the intended left turn. Then execute the next three right turns; you will then be going in the 'right' direction!

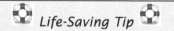 *Life-Saving Tip*

A LITTLE-KNOWN ADVISORY ABOUT LEFT TURNS

Except for very light traffic conditions, NEVER turn left across traffic from a point less than 50-100 yards from an intersection. If you are in traffic, do not make an opening for a car turning left within 50-100 yards of an intersection. Too often the car you let in is broadsided by a fast moving car in the center lane rushing to make a yellow light!

---

[4] The classic left-right-left also needs to include a view of what's ahead, so it's actually left-front-right-front-left. Pay attention to what's in front of you.

DRILL 3: U-TURNS ---

Let's face it, U-turns are dangerous, in many ways risky, similar to speeding: Like speeding, many drivers do it, it's generally dangerous, and we recommend against it. Like a pedestrian at an intersection, the U-turn it is often not expected.

 Maybe we could invent a U-turn indicator just like a regular turn signal. With that said, we want to give you and your teen the tools to succeed on this sometimes necessary maneuver.

✪ *Life-Saving Tip* ✪

What makes U-turns so dangerous?

- 👁 You can be hit head-on making a U-turn by a car travelling in the opposite direction that fails to notice you.

- 👁 You can be hit making a U-turn by a car on your left side as it travels straight ahead.

- 👁 You can be hit making a U-turn by a car on your left side that turns right, not seeing you.

- 👁 You can be hit making a U-turn by the car behind you that thinks you are simply turning left and not making a U-turn.

The Secrets of Safe U-Turns

Perform your U-turn drill on a wide residential street with little or no traffic and away from intersections. Always assume that other drivers do not see you. Finally, be aware that cars have different turning radiuses and sometimes you may not even be able to complete the U-turn without backing up the vehicle.

These are the potential problems to watch out for during U-turns:

- ☐ Oncoming vehicle running a red light.
- ☐ Vehicles turning right or left as you complete the U-turn.
- ☐ Traffic behind you moving fast as you set up the U-turn.
- ☐ U-turns on hills or curves.

The following exercises fulfill the drill:

Actual Drill

Depending on state traffic rules, you may perform a U-turn at one of two places: an intersection or in between intersections (mid-block). We are going to state: Never make a U-turn at an intersection—unless the

---

turn is controlled via traffic signals for a specific lane or you have a condition of zero traffic.

Preparation for the mid-block U-turn varies depending on the width of the road and the turning radius of your car. If at all possible, precede the U-turn by pulling onto the right shoulder of the road and stopping. Observe the following steps:

1) Check your mirrors and look over your left shoulder for traffic being clear behind you.

2) Look in front to verify no oncoming traffic.

3) Again check quickly behind you while activating your left turn signal, accelerating and turning about.

4) Glance in left mirror for traffic before pulling away.

If you cannot make the turn, don't force it. Just as in your state driver's test, do it in two more steps: Look L-R-L, then back up while turning the wheel clockwise, pause, look L-R-L, move forward and turn the wheel counterclockwise, and proceed in the opposite direction to which you were heading. Parent perform three, teen perform three.

DRILL 4: SURPRISE STOP ----------------------------------

Please take this moment to explain what a 'surprise stop' is before attempting. Your teen will be calling out "stop" as the parent is driving. Then the parent will call out stop as the teen is driving:

1) While driving straight, without any traffic behind or in the other lane of travel, and while traveling approximately 20 mph, have your teen loudly state "Stop" at any time (you will do it later when it's their turn to drive).

2) The driver should stop the vehicle in a straight line, without swerving left or right.

3) After three stops, switch seats and have your teen perform the drill, also three times.

Naturally, the preliminary surprise stop drill should be performed in light traffic areas. Overall, however, incorporate the 'surprise stop' into random driving... though never when stopping may cause an accident.

CULMINATION DRILL

Now have your teen do all four of the above drills, once each—Left Turn, Right Turn, U-Turn, and Surprise Stop—to demonstrate mastery.

Finally, enjoy the well-deserved 'Ice Cream Drill,' as described for Lesson 1 (page 23). Savor the moment. Well done!

 LIGHTER TURN

Never lend your vehicle to anyone to whom you have given birth. — Erma Bombeck

LESSON #3
'Dissecting' Intersections

TEEN STATISTIC

Did you know that in 2002, 3.2 million collisions occurred at intersections? This represents 50% of all reported crashes, 22% of all fatalities, and *a staggering cost of 100 billion dollars*. In 2009, more than 12,000 fatal crashes occurred at intersections.

Actual
FT KNOX
Vanity License Plates

Life-Saving Tip
Do not 'intersect' at an intersection ☺

Always slow down before entering an intersection AND assume that another driver may run a red light. Always scan Left-Right-Left.

What's That Definition?

Term	Meaning
Controlled Intersection	An intersection that has a stop light, stop sign or yield light, something that signals you to stop.
Uncontrolled Intersection	An intersection with no controls where the driver must determine when and if it's safe to proceed.

Lesson #3 Summary

What We Cover	Introduce your teen to driving through controlled and uncontrolled intersections, driving in moderate traffic. Entering intersections safely.
Location	Several places including intersections at city streets, business districts, and rural areas—where controlled and uncontrolled intersections exist—that are lightly trafficked to reduce the chance of collision.
Suggested Time	Weekend at noon. 45 to 60 minutes.

> 🛟 *Life-Saving Tip* 🛟
>
> *We choose a later time because drunk drivers may still be on the road from the night before. When someone drinks at night, falls asleep, and wakes up the next a.m. with a hangover, they are often still intoxicated.*

Speed Limits	Up to 50 mph, the legal limit or less when possible.
Parent Instruction	Before we start Drill 1, you the parent should drive to the lightly trafficked area you have chosen. Plan a travel route in advance where you both can operate the vehicle between 25 to 50 mph and have to stop and proceed through controlled and uncontrolled intersections. Explain the difference between controlled and uncontrolled intersections per the above definition table.

Q & A

Question: What makes intersections so dangerous?

Answer: The inability to see cars speeding, stopping or running red lights, and pedestrians walking.

DRILL 1: OBSERVING TRAFFIC LIGHTS WHILE PARKED

Both of you: park in a safe place near a busy intersection with a traffic light and spend the next 3-5 minutes actively watching the traffic light sequence. Count the number of drivers that go through the yellow sequence of the light or actually run a red light. While waiting, discuss in detail the importance of always slowing down before entering an intersection and looking Left-Right-Left.

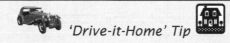 *'Drive-it-Home' Tip*

Remember that most collisions in city driving occur at intersections.

 NOTE

Perform the intersection drills in sequence according to the type of intersection control: 1) Stop Sign, 2) Yield Sign, 3) Traffic Light, 4) Uncontrolled. Parent will do first drill three times, then turn the wheel over to teen to perform first drill three times... then repeat procedure for second, third, and fourth drills.

DRILL 2: TRAVERSING A CONTROLLED INTERSECTION

You will traverse the following kinds of intersections:

Exercise 1: Stop Sign Intersection

Parent: you will demonstrate pulling up to one or more stop signs at controlled intersection(s) and coming to a complete stop—count to three seconds before proceeding. Second, stop at the white-painted lateral line, *not* at the stop sign itself. Third, proceed slowly into the intersection—ALWAYS PREPARE FOR ANY CAR FROM ANY DIRECTION TO RUN THE OTHTER STOP SIGNS. Look 'Left-Right-Left' before you enter.

Exercise 2: Yield Sign Intersection

Practice slowing down and stopping if necessary at a yield sign. Be on the lookout for cars entering that do not have the right of way. Proceed only when safe. Pay special attention to any traffic control devices. Stop when required. After stopping, check the view Left-Right-Left again before crossing the intersection.

Exercise 3: Traffic Light Intersections

Even though the light for you is green and you have the official right of way, explain the need to always proceed slowly and cautiously through an intersection. If you have stopped at the light, when it turns green start out slowly looking Left-Right-Left, watching for cars and expecting another driver to be entering the intersection. If you're entering a lighted intersection at speed, modulate your speed while looking L-R-L.

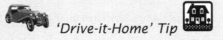

'Drive-it-Home' Tip

Keep your eyes moving! Check your mirrors! Look far and near!

Life-Saving Tip

If someone happens to be driving through a red light and headed into you for a potential disaster, prepare a plan of avoidance e.g., a) stopping quickly, b) steering out of the way, or c) accelerating away from the oncoming vehicle.

We suggest at this point, you pull over to a safe a quiet side street and let your teen navigate the above three types of controlled intersections at stop signs, yield signs, and traffic lights. Review the above information on each type. When your teen is finished with the third exercise, switch places on a quiet side street and drive to your next destination which will be an uncontrolled intersection.

⚠ CAUTION!

While you are stopped to make a left turn at an intersection or any point where oncoming traffic exists, do NOT turn the steering wheel to the left. A vehicle striking you from behind would push your car into oncoming traffic. Keep the tires pointed straight until making the turn.

DRILL 3: TRAVERSING AN UNCONTROLLED INTERSECTION

Parent: Your turn to drive. Find two or more intersections without traffic control devices. First, pull up to the intersection. Next, if no one is behind you, without allowing the front of the car to extend into the intersection, come to a complete stop. Check the view carefully looking

Left-Right-Left before crossing the intersection. Cross only when no traffic is close enough to present a hazard. Visit several intersections, perform the drill, then it's your teen's turn.

CULMINATION DRILL

Now have your teen do all four of the above drills, once each in succession—Stop Sign, Yield Sign, Traffic Light, Uncontrolled—to demonstrate mastery.

Finally, enjoy the well-deserved 'Ice Cream Drill,' as described for Lesson 1 (page 23). Savor the moment. Well done!

 NOTABLE QUOTE

Safety doesn't happen by accident. — Author Unknown

LESSON #4
Navigating Dangerous Intersections and Heavy Traffic

TEEN STATISTIC

Intersection collisions play a role in roughly 30% of all driving fatalities. Cars at intersections are travelling at rapid speeds in opposite directions without any protective barrier other than the car itself. If a mistake or a stop violation occurs, the results can be deadly. This lesson teaches how to handle intersections.

Lesson #4 Summary

What We Cover	Three-second spacing, safely navigating heavily trafficked intersections and defensive driving techniques.
Location	Busy city intersections and roadways. Bring a pad of paper and a pen to record Drill 1.

Suggested Time	The time that works best for you:
	❑ Friday night at 5-6 pm during moderately heavy traffic.
	❑ A weekday morning on a well travelled street on the way to school.
	❑ A weekend busy street (e.g. downtown, a shopping mall, a stadium, etc).
	Time required: Approx. 60 minutes. Repeat lesson if desired.
Speed Limits	City roadways with speeds up to 40 mph.
Parent Instruction	Drive to the area you have chosen in advance—a route which includes intersections and heavy city traffic. Parent completes each drill three times before teen performs them.

Question: What percentage of cars runs a red light?

Answer: We believe this would be a great study topic and believe the figure to be about 10-15% of drivers. Let's find out.

Question: How many seconds should you leave in front of you?

Answer: Three seconds… more with increased speed or dangerous conditions present.

NOTE

Be sure to practice some older drills and call out a few 'surprise stops.'

DRILL 1: OBSERVING A TRAFFIC LIGHT --------------------

Obtain a pen and a pad of paper. You or your teen will pull the car safely over to the side of a busy road near a traffic light and spend the next five minutes observing and documenting the light sequences of the traffic light.

❑ First, have your teen record the number of seconds that the yellow light is activated before changing to red.

❑ Next, count the seconds it takes for the light to turn red and then green.

Finally, discuss with your teen the following questions:

❑ Why did the city engineers who created the light sequencing choose the timing for any given pattern?

❑ Why is the yellow light the shortest? What happens if someone runs the yellow or red light?

❑ What should you do if someone runs the yellow or red light?

❑ Should you go immediately when the light turns green? Why not?

Now we suggest driving to two more lights and timing their sequence pattern as well. Hint: travel to an area that is much more or much less heavily trafficked. The light sequence most likely will be different because it is based in part on the count of cars passing by daily.

Have your teen document each traffic light sequence and ask, 'Is the traffic light sequence any different if the road is heavily travelled? Is the timing related to speed limit? Did you notice anything about the intersection and why the engineers chose this pattern? If you were the engineer, what would you do to make the intersection safer?

DRILL 2: 'THE THREE-SECOND CHALLENGE --------------

🔘 *Life-Saving Tip* 🔘

Having a safe space cushion—think of an astronaut having a space suit—is one of the best defensive driving techniques to help your teen avoid being harmed in a serious accident.

A space cushion means maintaining space on each side of your car directly to your left, right, front, and back so you have a 'cushion' or space available in an emergency. For example, what happens if the car in front of you stops immediately? With an adequate cushion, you avoid the collision. Similarly, if someone enters your lane, leave yourself a space to change lanes. We need to anticipate what other drivers may do.

A space cushion means maintaining space on each side of your car directly to your left, right, front, and back so you have a 'cushion' or space available in an emergency.

Mostly, avoiding collisions requires safe, timely stopping. Your car is massive and takes seconds to stop at best. Experience shows that a space cushion of three seconds or more between you and the car in front provides a practical 'margin of error' that saves lives. "A collision is no accident." Understand and execute the following three-second drill—leaving a space cushion on the sides and back as well:

1) Parent: proceed in normal traffic demonstrating the 'three-second following-distance rule' from the car ahead.

2) While driving, identify a car for this drill that is in front of you by its color and make-if you know it. Drive behind this car at a safe driving distance of about three seconds.

3) To determine the number of seconds you are behind, have your teen do the following: wait for the car in front to pass a fixed point such as a sign or street pole, then count the  seconds—one-thousand-one, one-thousand-two, one-thousand-three…—it takes your car to reach this spot. Were you a driving distance of three seconds or more? Ultimately, keeping distances helps you take a big bite out of Litigation Nation. ☺

4) Next, identify a different vehicle and safely adjust your distance so that you are travelling at a longer or shorter distance.[5] Your teen counts the seconds again.

5) When it is safe, pull over and have your teen perform the drill. This enables your teen to see the proper three seconds needed in normal traffic conditions.

Higher speeds or rain or snow conditions demand a greater interval between cars, say, 5-8 seconds. Universal adoption of the three-second rule would lower collisions and fatalities substantially. Next time you're in the passenger seat on an expressway, estimate how many drivers adhere to the three-second rule. It may be a sobering discovery. ☹

DRILL 3: INTERSECTIONS, HEAVY TRAFFIC ------

Parent: now it is your turn to demonstrate how to safely approach and traverse heavily trafficked intersections:

---

[5] Your goal should be to maintain a distance from the car in front of you between two and three seconds for normal driving conditions. Below two is dangerously close, above three is not keeping with the flow of traffic.

1) Enter the right lane of travel if there is more than one lane.

2) Slow down before the intersection and continually look Left-Right-Left, even if the light is green.

3) Maintain a safe following distance in front and behind you obeying all traffic control devices.

4) Carefully observe all street signs, roadway markings, crossing traffic, parked or stopped vehicles, pedestrians, and turning traffic.

5) Continue to drive in heavy traffic and practice changing lanes in between (before approaching) intersections.

6) Incorporate turns and lane changes making sure to maintain a proper sight picture, space cushion, and use of the turn signals.

After about 10 minutes of driving, pull over to a safe place and have your teen perform the drill.

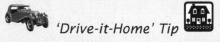

'Drive-it-Home' Tip

Always scan 'Left-Right-Left' when entering an intersection. You never know when a speeding car will run a red or yellow light.

Ask your teen what they learned about travelling in busy intersections and the differences between uncrowded intersections and regular city streets.

DRILL 4: DEFENSIVE DRIVING DRILL ----------------------

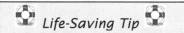

Life-Saving Tip

A great defensive driver anticipates potential hazards. It's always vital to be on the lookout for 'what might and could happen.' Imagine and then practice different scenarios to improve your awareness, as outlined in the subdrills below. Pretend practice in these drills which can help perfect driving skills in actual unforeseen driving situations.

For these drills, we recommend using a street with less traffic so that you can leave even more space on all sides of the car. Practice makes perfect and practicing emergencies helps make your teen a safer and more aware driver.

DRILL 4A ---

Pretend a car is stopping immediately in front of you in an intersection due to an emergency.

As you, the parent, are driving with no cars present, have your teen call out to you that a pretend car in front of you is stopping NOW. You will rapidly slow down the vehicle and perform these steps:

a) Analyze the situation.

b) Slow down as fast as possible.

c) Determine if you should change lanes; do so only if you cannot avoid hitting the car in front of you.

d) If you decide to change lanes, check for cars.

Otherwise, changing lanes can be more deadly than avoiding the initial situation and this is why you must drive at a safe speed to have time to react safely.

📝 IMPORTANT!

Never 'slam' on the brakes in a panic. Even in the most immediate emergency, quickly move your foot and firmly apply the brakes NOW. It is never a SLAM. A slam can cause your foot to slip off the brake pedal. The immediate stop drill is very important to practice stopping quickly and EFFECTIVELY.

DRILL 4B ---

Pretend that a small animal runs into the road in front of you.

While you are safely driving, with no cars present, have your teen call out that a skunk or other small animal has run into your lane. Here's what to do:

a) Engage a nose plug. ☺ [We know, not very funny.]

b) Analyze the situation.

c) Slow down rapidly making sure not to hit any other cars.

d) Can you change lanes to avoid hitting the animal?

e) If so, check for cars before making the lane change.

f) Don't 'duck' your critter-avoidance responsibilities. ☺

🛟 *Life-Saving Tip* 🛟

Remember every emergency maneuver or braking can cause a fatal, unintended consequence if you are following too closely.

DRILL 4C --

Pretend a small object like a rock is coming at you.

As you drive along safely, with no cars present, have your teen call out that an object—say, a rock or an uprooted bush— is flying toward you. Use the steps in 4B to  avoid this. Note if the object is small, weighs little, is not living, and will not cause you or your car serious harm, letting the object strike the car may be your best choice.

⚠ CAUTION!

Prepare for emergency situations. Simply reacting quickly can create a new and more dangerous condition. As in football, know when to punt and when to go for it.

DRILL 4D --

Pretend at an intersection that a car has run the red light and is heading straight toward you.

At a very lightly travelled intersection with no cars present, your teen will say a car is running the red and is coming straight at you for a head-on collision. Take these avoidance steps:

a) Instantly analyze the situation.

b) Slow down as fast as possible, not hitting any cars.

c) Can you change lanes to avoid hitting the car head on?

🛟 *Life-Saving Tip* 🛟

Head on collisions are the most dangerous of all collisions. Try anything to avoid a head-on collision including steering your car away from the other car.

d) As a last resort, honk your horn aggressively, speed up, swerve out of the way, brake utmost hard, or use any behavior you can think of to avoid hitting the car. The goal is to avoid at all costs a head-on collision even if it means driving to the side of the road. (Do watch for pedestrians though.)

Now it is your teen's turn to conquer the Drills 4A-4D. Ideally have your teen perform each drill three times as follows: Drill 4a: three times; Drill 4b: three times, etc. Teen, Drills 1-3 may be performed as often as desired, but do each of them at least once.

CULMINATION DRILL

Now your teen will perform Drills 2 through 4 in succession to demonstrate mastery.

 Finally, enjoy the well-deserved 'Ice Cream Drill,' as described for Lesson 1 (page 23). Savor the moment. Well done!

 LIGHTER TURN

Never drive faster than your guardian angel can fly.
— Author unknown

LESSON #5
Freeway Driving Made Easy

The following percentages of fatalities are based on the specific driver behavior listed below:[6]

- ☐ 53% were not wearing seatbelts.
- ☐ 40% were alcohol related.
- ☐ 34% were speed related.
- ☐ 21% occurred at intersections.
- ☐ 14% were pedestrians.
- ☐ 12% were motorcycle riders.
- ☐ 1% were bicycle riders.

Note that many of these dangerous activities happened simultaneously since the numbers add up to more than 100%.

Q & A

Question: What do the top three statistics above illustrate?

Answer: They show that poor judgment—not wearing seat belts, *drinking and driving*, or speeding—is associated with an astounding number of road fatalities.

---

[6] From Massachusetts Crash Fatality Roadway Safety Facts, 2006

NOTE

The most significant association (and one that surprised us) is that 53% of all fatalities were related to the drivers or passengers not wearing seatbelts.

Lesson #5 Summary

What We Cover	Entering the freeway, driving on the freeway and getting off the freeway as easy as 1-2-3.
Location	Thoroughfares with very sparse traffic.
Suggested Time	Weekend mornings about 8:30 a.m. Repeat drill as needed.
Speed Limits	Up to 65 mph.
Parent Instruction	Use these drills, including the oral discussion, to enable your teen to handle freeway driving with competence and authority.

Parent completes each drill three times first then the teen driver completes the drill three times.

DRILL 1: ORAL DRILL ON FREEWAY DRIVING

Hold a discussion on the following:

Table 3: Oral Drill on Freeway Driving

#	Issue	Answer
1	Ask your teen what is the proper method for entering a freeway.	Check your intended lane of entry to see if you can merge into it safely; obey the traffic signs and activate turn indicator; merge by entering and accelerating smoothly to traffic speed.
2	Which of the following is easier and generally safer to drive on: a freeway/expressway or a city street?	Most collisions occur at intersections on city streets so statistically speaking the safer place to drive is on the freeway. In fact, the majority of all collisions occur within two miles of your home on city streets. But freeways do present three real dangers: ☐ changing lanes ☐ hitting a car in front or being hit from behind ☐ the higher speeds you travel Thus, any collision impact is generally is very dangerous due to the kinetic energy of contact.

#	Issue	Answer
3	Ask your teen if they know how freeway lanes are numbered and what is the safest lane to travel on.	The freeway numbering system is unusual, yet easy to remember. The lanes are numbered in progression with the first lane being the fastest and the last lane being the slow lane. If there are four lanes, the fast lane is Lane 1 while the slow lane is Lane 4.
		The safest lanes are generally considered the middle lanes (Lane 2 and Lane 3 in the above four-lane freeway). Fewer lane changes are required and speeds are less than in the fast lane.

DRILL 2: ENTERING AND EXITING THE FREEWAY---------

General info before you begin:

Many drivers—not only beginners—are fearful at the prospect of ten lanes, five in each direction, of traffic moving at high speeds. Freeway traffic is usually light on Sunday morning and it's a good time to give your teen their first taste of freeway driving—after initially watching you enter the freeway three times.

Don't worry, spaghetti is the exception. 😊

Note to your teen that freeway driving is the safest and easiest place to drive once they get the feel for it, which is why it is called a freeway— you can travel on it for a long time without having to stop or change lanes. They enter by first checking their mirrors and glancing over their shoulders to find an opening. After entering stay in the same lane for a few miles, exiting is a breeze: check mirrors, turn on signal, slow down.

✎ NOTE

Choose a freeway section that has several exits close to one another, so if you miss one, the next one is imminent:

Entering the Freeway in 10 Easy Steps

1) From the time you begin driving to when you enter the on-ramp for the freeway, note all posted signs.

2) As you enter the on-ramp, turn on your left turn signal.

---

3) When the ramp is clear, accelerate to gain enough speed to match the flow of traffic.

4) Before entering the freeway, glance left to make sure you can enter there. For example, there could be a hill or bump on your left side blocking your entrance point. [Trust us on that one... it happened to one of the authors as a teenager. ☺]

5) Check left hand and center rearview mirrors for cars in your way, accelerating, decelerating as necessary. [Don't worry, you can always slow down, stop, or pull over to the right shoulder in the rare case you are completely blocked.]

6) As you merge into traffic, *do a final check* by glancing over your left shoulder for that occasional car that 'comes out of nowhere' (often changing lanes at high speed).

7) Straighten the car and stay in the right lane for awhile. Congratulations, you're on the freeway and headed straight!

8) Get your bearings, cancel the turn indicator, check your mirrors quickly and carefully for nearby cars.

9) Quickly check that a car in front is not slowing rapidly. Remember to leave your space cushions all around.

10) Drive in the same lane for a while; when comfortable engage your right turn signal and exit the freeway.

Exiting the Freeway in 5 Easy Steps

1) Relax, take your time. Remember it is easier exiting than entering. Ready? Turn on your right turn indicator.

2) Look in the right mirror first and then check the rear view mirror for any cars... which may be entering the freeway as you are exiting.

3) Glance over your right hand shoulder for any cars.

4) Quickly but steadily exit the freeway, then slow the vehicle paying close attention to any car in front. If the light is red at the bottom of the ramp, you must be prepared to stop—change speed from 60 mph to zero—in roughly 15 seconds.

5) Prepare to stop at the light or stop sign on the exit road.

Parent completes each drill three times first then the teen driver completes the drill three times. The detailed instructions above are written for the new driver's benefit

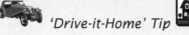

'Drive-it-Home' Tip

Slower traffic keeps to the right.

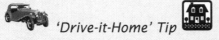

'Drive-it-Home' Tip

A car travelling on the freeway in the right lane has the right-of-way over a vehicle driving up the on-ramp.

Parent: when your teen has mastered entering and exiting the freeway, take over the wheel again for our next drill. Drill 3 is similar to Drill 2, but with a twist—you will change lanes every mile or two, multiple times over the next 10-15 minutes.

DRILL 3: ENTERING FREEWAY AND CHANGING LANES

Proceed as follows:

1) Parent: enter the freeway safely using the steps in Drill 2. Stay in the slow lane at first.

2) Before changing freeway lanes, always check in front of you first to see if any cars are slowing quickly. Stay relaxed and comfortable.

3) Turn on your left turn indicator.

4) Check your left hand and rear mirrors mirror for traffic and glance over your left shoulder to change lanes.

5) Change lanes into the gap and straighten out your car.

6) Make sure the car in front hasn't slowed down.

7) Drive in this new lane for a mile, then change lanes again (to the left).

8) Change lanes every mile or so, eventually moving into the fastest lane (Lane 1). Then move to the slower lanes, using your right mirror and glancing over your right shoulder.

9) Exit the freeway.

After performing this drill three times, have your teen also perform the drill three times.

CULMINATION DRILL

Now your teen will perform Drills 2 and 3 in succession to demonstrate mastery.

Finally, enjoy the well-deserved 'Ice Cream Drill,'—or a warm cup of marshmallow hot chocolate—as described for Lesson 1 (page 23). Savor the moment. Well done!

 LIGHTER TURN

Car sickness is the feeling you get when the monthly payment is due. — Anonymous

---

LESSON #6
Night Driving... Like a Star

TEEN STATISTIC

 The Royal Society for the Prevention of Accidents (Great Britain) states that night driving is the most dangerous, accounting for 40% of all accidents—significant because fewer people drive at night. Why? Vision is impaired at night. Also, people tend to fall asleep at night. In fact, 20% of all serious accidents involve drivers falling asleep. Yikes! Never let your teen drive if they are not rested.

In Lesson 5, your teen learned the proper method for entering and exiting freeways and the proper techniques for changing lanes on a freeway or expressway. In Lesson 6 we use many of the past drills, performing them at night.

Lesson #6 Summary

What We Cover	Every aspect of night time driving.
Location	All previous lesson routes.

Traffic Safety Consultants, Inc.   *45*

Suggested Time	Any 'starry' night when the roads are quiet and clear. 60 minutes. Repeat the lesson if needed.
Speed Limits	Up to 65 mph. (Preferably less than the speed limit.)
Parent Instruction	States with graduated licensing laws require parents to practice at least 10 hours of night driving with their teen. Start after your teen has mastered daytime driving. This lesson is a series of basic nighttime driving drills.

📝 NOTE

Bring a pad and pencil for our observation drills. Many drills here will take place at both a.m. and p.m. Either order is fine.

Most states make it illegal to drive too fast for conditions. Darkness reduces visibility, so always slow down when driving at night, regardless of the posted speed limit or traffic. Parent completes each drill three times first then the teen driver completes the drill three times.

DRILL 1: ORAL DISCUSSION DRILL

Discuss the following with your teen:

1) Why is night driving more dangerous than daytime driving?

Answer: Vision is reduced making it tougher to see hazards and react correctly. Also, humans are biologically programmed to sleep at night when vision is worst.

2) Are there more or fewer cars on the road at night?

Answer: Even though we find fewer cars on the road at night— which would seem to make driving safer—night time driving is more dangerous because of impaired vision.

> 🛟 *Life-Saving Tip* 🛟
>
> *Call 911 when you note someone swerving or driving erratically, often drunk. It's a free call that may save a life... or six.*

3) Since vision is impaired, how can we drive more safely?

Answer: Look farther ahead. Always scan the distance. Check your mirrors frequently and anticipate any potential hazards such as animals entering the road or *on* the road.

Always be aware of potential drunk/wrong way drivers. If you spot a drunk driver—they tend to swerve between lanes continually while travelling either very fast or slow—be a Good Samaritan and safely pull off the road to call 911. Such efforts may save someone's life.

One of the few safety benefits of modern day cell phones is instead of having one watchful eye: you now have thousands of drivers self-policing potential drunk driving. The real deterrent? Teens don't want to end up on YouTube seen being arrested for a DUI. ☺

4) Why must our car's headlights be maintained?

Answer: Headlights illuminate objects allowing you to see clearer at a distance. If one or more headlights are broken, have them replaced immediately. Broken headlights are a safety hazard; the police may pull you over for an infraction—a so-called fixit ticket.

5) What is proper use of high-beam and low-beam lamps?

Answer: Use normal low-beam lights in general. When it's dark or difficult to see, turn on your high beams; instantly turn off the high beams when another car approaches. High beams can temporarily blind an oncoming driver due to their wider and higher angle. [They can also blind the driver going your way in front of you.]

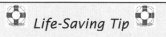 *Life-Saving Tip*

Never use your high beams in fog, rain, or snow because they will increase light reflection, actually making it harder to see.

---

6) Name two or more dangerous nighttime driving situations both inside and outside of the car.

Answer:

☐ Drivers at night do not see your car as easily.

☐ Animals are more likely to be on the road at night.

☐ The driver does not see smaller objects as well.

☐ Pedestrians are difficult to see.

☐ Street signs, addresses, and speed limit signs are more difficult to see.

☐ Items in your car—especially controls for stereo, lights, heating and cooling—are tougher to use.

Most important, *drunk and wrong-way drivers are far more plentiful at night than during the day*, making night driving especially hazardous.

The following drill compares time of day driving conditions.

DRILL 2: NIGHT DRIVING VS. DAY DRIVING --------------

For this fun drill, we ask that you bring your pen, a pad of paper, and a stopwatch (with a flashlight). If you do not have a stopwatch, simply estimate the times required to spot items during the day vs. night. Perform each of these drills once during the day and once at night.

How long does it take to see three separate objects in daylight vs. night? During the day, first, and then later at night, on the same exact street, the parent will drive to a quiet street and your teen will write down how far and/or how long it takes them to see each of the three items below at their soonest point of contact:

1) a dark-colored car driving on the road
2) a street sign name
3) a speed sign that has an 'mph' on it

Proceed as follows:

1) First, parent, determine the approximate distance and time it takes at both a.m. and p.m. to spot *a dark-colored car* that is stopped at a red light and then mark down the approximate distance and/or time in seconds it takes you to identify the car.

2) Next, try to determine how long it takes and/or estimate the distance required to correctly read a *street sign* during the day and then for the same sign on a very dark, unlit area at night.

3) Finally, time and/or estimate the distance when you can first see *an 'mph' sign* during the day and later at night.

The difference will be significant. When finished, review your results together and discuss your teen's conclusions. What steps can be taken to help your teen become a safer driver at night? Now let's continue our experiment… with some more drills.

Observing a Busy Intersection

During the day, and later at night, parent park your car in a safe area close to a busy intersection for observation. Have your teen estimate and write down, for day and night conditions:

a) The approximate rate of speed that most vehicles travel through the intersection.

b) The approximate time it takes for the average driver to stop at the intersection when first encountering a red light.

c) How many drivers out of 10 have difficultly stopping at a red light?

d) Which is worse for the driver: i) the sun's glare during the day or ii) the glare of other cars' lights while other cars proceed through the intersection.

Discuss your findings. Here are some questions:

1) Did your teen observe any differences with the visibility of a car during the day vs. the night?

2) Discuss the problems of nighttime glare and other dangers from oncoming vehicles' headlights can cause.

3) Consider buying and actually wearing quality sun glasses during the day to remove sun glare and help you see better.

4) Discuss how long it takes for one's eyes to adjust after being 'blinded' by an oncoming vehicle's high beams.

Next we are going to embark on a few night time only drills.

DRILL 3: BASIC DRIVING DRILL (AT NIGHT) ---------------

You and your teen will now take a comprehensive nighttime drive thru:

a) a quiet residential street

b) a quiet business street

c) right, left, and U-turns on business streets

d) freeway driving at night

Please do one section at a time as outlined exactly below.

a) *Night Driving on a Quiet Residential Street*

You (parent) drive to a quiet residential area. While driving, both of you scan the road and area ahead for potential hazards and any movement, including:

☐ cars backing up out of the driveway

☐ cars turning

☐ pedestrians walking

☐ children playing

☐ cars without lights or broken lights

Point out that cars generally, but not always, have working lights turned on. So usually when a car backs up you see the rear red lights as an indicator of that motion. After 7-10 minutes of driving, pull over and let your teen drive.

b) *Night Driving on Quiet Business Street*

Parent, proceed to drive to a quiet business district. First, drive straight ahead for a few miles. Leave plenty of room and braking distance for stop signs and so on. Point out to your teen the potential hazards you see such as those in the bulleted list above.

Then, pull over safely and let your teen drive on a business street for several miles straight ahead for a few miles, just as you the parent did.

Have your teen pull over to a safe area away from traffic, then discuss their thoughts on night driving. Is it easy? Hard? Fun? Challenging? Challenging and Fun? Are they ready to progress to more difficult maneuvers such as making turns and finally driving on the freeway at night? Remind them they need to be extra cautious at night since other drivers cannot see them as well.

c) *Intermediate Night Driving; Right Turns, Left Turns, and U-Turns*

Now, parent, are you ready to show your teen that you are a star? Okay, let's practice turns: 1) three right turns, 2) three left turns, 3) three U-turns explaining to your teen the basics:

a) press the turn indicator on

b) slow down

c) watch for cars/pedestrians before turning

d) proceed only when safe

You may take this opportunity to review the exact instructions for each turn maneuver as listed in Lesson 2 (taking into account night-driving conditions).

When the parent finishes, pull over to a safe spot and have your teen make the right/left/U-turns where safe and legal. Ask your teen about the difficulties in seeing cars, street signs, lights, and pedestrians at night.

Finally it is time to demonstrate the final drill for freeway driving: advanced night driving.

d) Advanced Night Driving—Freeway/Expressway

The final drill is a critical one, to be able to drive at night with the higher speeds and lowered visibility. Remember, ALWAYS pay attention, more so at night.

 NOTE

You may want to review the past lesson on entering a freeway during the daytime and apply that lesson to freeway driving at night.

Parent, drive to and enter a freeway using the two drills outlined below. Perform each of the drills three times before having your teen perform them.

1) Practice entering the freeway and travelling straight ahead at night for a few miles before exiting. For this drill, do *not* make any lane changes on the freeway.

2) The second freeway drill is to enter the freeway at night and change lanes every mile or so until you reach the fast lane (Lane 1). Then, one lane at a time, progress back to the slow lane, and exit the freeway. [Same as previous chapter.]

   Pay special attention to scanning ahead, maintaining proper following distance, and making proper lane changes. Are you leaving a space cushion?

Query your teen how to enter the freeway and change lanes. Now have them practice entering the freeway and travelling straight before exiting. Second, they will enter the freeway and change lanes as described in step 2 of Subdrill d above. Their time to be a 'star.'

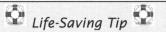 *Life-Saving Tip*

What lane do wrong way drunk drivers drive in at night? Drunk drivers frequently cannot distinguish between a freeway 'entrance' or 'exit.' Thus they frequently drive up the exit beginning their deadly journey going the wrong way. Once they have entered the freeway, they change lanes rapidly, accelerate, and then drive in the fastest lane (your Lane #1). Thus it's best to avoid driving in Lane 1 at night. Pretend every time you crest a hill that an obstacle or wrong-way driver awaits you.

CULMINATION DRILL

Perform the drills above the number of times per the instruction within each drill. In this culmination drill your teen performs all the driving drills in succession to demonstrate mastery.

Now enjoy the well-deserved 'Ice Cream Drill,' or a hot chocolate or apple cider, etc., as described for Lesson 1 (page 23). Savor the moment. Well done!

 **LIGHTER TURN**

Another way to solve the traffic problems in this country is to pass a law that only vehicles that are paid for will be allowed to use the highways. — Will Rogers

Lesson #7
Haven't the Foggiest
Hazardous Weather Conditions

TEEN STATISTIC

Researcher Daniel Eisenberg showed the more it rains or snows monthly that 3.7% fewer fatal collisions occur. Collisions rise in rain or snow, but fatalities actually drop since, he theorized, *higher speeds have higher death rates* and drivers as a whole compensate for bad conditions by slowing down.

The way some people drive, the car should be considered an accomplice.

Lesson #7 Summary

What We Cover	Drills on how to navigate dangerous driving conditions.
Location	Depending on where you live, you may not have the opportunity to have your teen drive in snow or icy roads. However, operating a car in rain, fog, or any poor-driving condition helps prepare them to drive safely in all hazardous conditions.
Suggested Time	When bad weather strikes. 60 minutes.
Speed Limits	Slower speeds and extreme caution.
Parent Instruction	Practice these drills only when your teen has a minimum of 40 hours with you in clear conditions.

 **IMPORTANT**

We strongly suggest that you and your teen take this moment to now discuss every hazardous condition outlined below because you may not get an opportunity to drill on each condition. Practice these drills orally now until the weather strikes and you can pull out the book.

When the poor weather condition occurs, pull out our guidebook and do the drills. You only have a short time window to teach your teen to drive… and stay alive. Our natural inclination is to hope that our teens never have to drive in poor conditions. But they will, so preparation can definitely save their bacon.

DRILL 1: DRIVING IN RAIN ------------------------------------

Before driving in the rain, discuss how rain:

- ☐ severely reduces visibility

- ☐ requires a greater stopping distance

- ☐ increases the importance of keeping both hands on the wheel

- ☐ means using your car's normal, low-beam headlights

- ☐ makes it necessary to properly use the car's windshield wipers and window defrosters, for visibility

- ☐ increases the possibility of *hydroplaning*

⚑ DEFINITION

Hydroplaning is when a car's tires ride above the road's surface and the tires have trouble gripping the road as a layer of water comes between the road and the car.

Rain makes it difficult to turn a car quickly without skidding, so you need to drive slowly, avoid rapid turns, and avoid rapid braking. Discuss whether or not your car has antilock brakes—hint: look in your car manual under brakes—which help securely slow the vehicle in the rain. Also whether you have stability traction control to automatically steer the car on loss of control by slowing the car and correcting the steering.

❖ Life-Saving Tip ❖

The NHTSA estimates that stability traction control saves approximately 11,000 lives a year. If you don't have it on your car, we urge you to trade in your car for a five-star rated car that has both anti-lock brakes and stability traction control (ref. www.safercar.gov).

Subdrills A and B will be driving drills, but if there is no rain do the drills pretending you are under rain conditions.

A) Slowing in the Rain Drill

First, you (the parent) will drive to an open and deserted road or highway, driving only straight ahead in the rain. Get a feel for driving in the rain and the level of attention and care such driving requires.

When safe and when no cars are present. at a very slow speed at no more than 10 mph and then later at 15 mph, demonstrate our drill by slowing the car methodically to 5 mph and 10 mph, respectively. Be careful to not make a sudden stop or turn with the wheel. Did your car stop slowly or did it slide a little?

✎ NOTE

If your car has anti-lock brakes, you will practice pushing down on the vehicle brake pedal slowly and maintaining firm pressure on the pedal until the vehicle comes to a complete stop.

NOTE

In the unlikely event that your car enters a minor skid at a slow speed, simply correct the front end of the car while casually steering your vehicle straight ahead.

B) Making Turns in the Rain

Parent, after successfully completing the above braking drills, please proceed to making safe right turns, left turns and U-turns, also slowing down and using extra precaution in the rain.

At a safe place, please exit the car and let your teen take control and do the above drills three times or more. When finished, you may go for ice cream or hot chocolate, but maybe have your 'scoops' at home!

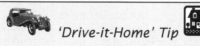 *'Drive-it-Home' Tip*

The most dangerous time to drive in the rain is the first 30 minutes. The road is extremely slippery because the oil and grease have come up off the pavement. After a while the rain washes the 'slick' away. A particularly treacherous rain is a light drizzle—because not enough rain is coming down to wash the 'slick' away.

DRILL 2: DRIVING IN SNOW OR ICE (PRETEND-PRACTICE IF NECESSARY)

Driving in snow, like driving in the rain, requires similar safe driving techniques of Drill 1. Driving in the snow is probably more difficult due to the colder weather and the difficulty of your car's normal tires in gripping the road. Before doing the snow-driving drills, review the above rain-driving drills.

1) Oral discussion: Before driving, discuss how snow reduces visibility, requires a greater stopping distance, the importance of keeping both hands on the wheel, the need to use your car's normal, low-beam headlights, and use of the heater and defroster. Discuss black ice conditions:

DEFINITION: BLACK ICE

Black Ice is an area of ice which is often impossible to see.
When you drive over this slippery ice patch, it may cause
your car to lose control.

Should you encounter black ice, take your foot off the gas pedal, *slowly* depress the brakes while simultaneously correcting the front of the car in a skid.

2) Install snow tires and/or chains, if available. Demonstrate or discuss the method of installing snow tires and/or snow chains before driving. If you don't own them, we suggest reading more about them online or asking your local service station personnel for a demonstration of how they work.

3) Stop in the snow at 5 mph and 10 mph, in turn. When finished, have your teen do the same, three times or as needed.

4) Practice right turns, left turns, and U-turns slowly in the snow. Parents, demonstrate each condition first, followed by your teen, three times.

Why is it that, when you're driving and looking for an address,
you turn down the volume on the radio?

 Ice Cream Drill: Usually we suggest that when finished, you head out for ice cream, but here we would recommend that you grab a nice hot chocolate or apple cider in the comfort and warmth of the fireplace in your living room. Just an idea.

⚠ CAUTION!

Some winter roads are in sun and shade. Ice will form in shady
stretches of road first because of the lower air temperature.

DRILL 3: DRIVING IN WIND (PRETEND-PRACTICE IF NECESSARY)

Before driving in the wind, spend a few minutes on an oral drill discussing how the wind:

☐ reduces driver visibility

☐ increases the need for stopping distances

☐ can sometimes move a car or cause difficulty in steering

☐   can send objects hurtling at your car

 NOTE

All the above conditions are more severe at higher speeds. Wind also makes it imperative to keep both hands firmly on the steering wheel.

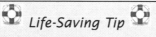 *Life-Saving Tip*

Consider planning ahead and partially activating the window defroster and/or heater in advance when you anticipate windy conditions. Under the stress of trying to see and steer in the wind, your body temperature will rise significantly and combine with air moisture creating foggy windows.

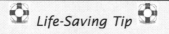 *Life-Saving Tip*

When visibility drops to near zero, pull off to the far side of the road; get out of harm's way rather than hit a stopped driver ahead of you or be hit from behind.

Proceed as follows:

Parent, take a drive in windy weather first before turning over your car to your teen. After approximately 10 minutes of driving straight ahead and getting comfortable, demonstrate the stopping drill outlined in Drill 1 of rain driving above.

After the stopping drill, it's time to conquer right turns, left turns, and U-turns in the wind. When safe, pull over and have your teen practice (three times each) driving as Bob Seger once wrote, 'against the wind.'

 We frequently suggest that when finished with a lesson that you head out for ice cream, but may we suggest a nice hot chocolate or apple cider in the warmth of your living room fireplace.

DRILL 4: DRIVING IN FOG (OR PRETEND PRACTICE IF NECESSARY)

Like driving in the wind, fog presents the driver with a series of difficult challenges, mainly seeing objects in front or behind you. Vision is seriously impaired if the fog is dense. Discuss with your teen how fog affects driving in the following ways:

☐   lower visibility

- [ ] greater stopping distance
- [ ] less reaction time
- [ ] difficulty seeing
- [ ] extra importance of keeping both hands on the wheel
- [ ] the need to use low-beam lights
- [ ] the prudent use of window wipers and car defoggers/heaters

Also you need to pull over to a safe and secure area off the road when visibility nears zero.

The fog drill is the same as the rain drill (#1 above). So, parent drive straight ahead slowly. Next, when you have adequate spacing in traffic, do your braking drills. Then finish with performing right turns, left turns, and U-turns. Turn the wheel over to your teen to have them perform the same drill.

We suggest, when finished, you celebrate with a root beer float or whatever is your 'cup of tea.'

DRILL 5: DRIVING IN HAIL (OR PRETEND PRACTICE IF NECESSARY)

Due to hail's relative rarity, you and your teen may never have an opportunity to practice this drill. So if it happens at all, you go for a 'Hail' Mary, as in football. ☺ For now, discuss orally the techniques for driving in hail: how hail causes low visibility, requires greater stopping

distance, results in less reaction time. [Note: You definitely will not want to drive in a hailstorm like the one on the left.]

Hail, as the other weather hazards, requires you to keeping both hands on the wheel. Be prepared in advance and to activate your car's window wipers, heaters, and defrosters. Also, use normal, 'low beam' headlights. Should the hail become overwhelming, pull over to the right side of the road safely until the hail ends.

If the opportunity presents itself, take your careful drive in hail using the drill steps identified for Drill #1: Rain Driving. Parent drives first slowly straight ahead. Practice stopping at various speeds, then graduate to right turns, left turns, and finally U-turns. Then have your teen drive in the hail performing the exercises three times each if conditions allow.

 We suggest, when finished, you celebrate by watching a Hail Mary pass during a football game together on your TV, have some s'mores, a hot pizza. And some hot chocolate. Or go to a local bar—only parents drinking, of course—and 'hail' a taxi home. ☺

CULMINATION DRILL

The culmination drill here is different: Anytime, if one of the above conditions presents itself, review our book and practice the corresponding drill several times. Practice makes perfect, and you need to be perfect in dangerous driving conditions. Okay, okay, you still get to do the Ice Cream Drill.

 ICE CREAM DRILL

Congratulations! You were both outstanding and now it's off to ice cream or yogurt, coffee, dinner or desert. You both earned it so go ahead and savor the moment.

 LIGHTER TURN

Teenagers complain there's nothing to do, then they stay out all night doing it. — Bob Phllips

LESSON #8
Emerging from Emergencies
TEEN STATISTIC

The NHTSA estimates that 1.5 million auto-deer accidents (collisions involving deer) occur annually at a cost of $1.5 billion. More disturbing, 150 people die from such accidents every year.

Emergencies are similar to driving under bad-weather conditions except that in bad weather, you can usually see the poor conditions develop first. Emergencies happen in the blink of an eye. Let's be prepared to handle them effectively.

Lesson #8 Summary

What We Cover	Handing emergencies so your teen is well prepared.
Location	An empty parking lot or low-traffic road.
Suggested Time	Day or night, when clear and safe, and with few cars. 60 minutes. Or more time as practice is needed.
Speed Limits	Speeds adjusted for the listed condition.
Parent Instruction	Have your teen drive for this drill but tell them that this is practice and not an actual emergency.

Alternatively, practice these 'emergencies' in the living room. However, practicing each emergency, pretending they happen while you drive, is more effective.

DRILL 1: HOOD FLIES OPEN --------------------------------

Do the actual drill by popping open the hood and trying to drive in a parking lot.

Before you start, ask your teen what they would do if the car's hood opened suddenly. Here are the steps to follow should the driver's view be impaired—maybe even mud on the front window:

1) Stay calm and peek in the crack between the hood and the car.

2) Still peeking thru the crack, bring the car to a complete stop. If possible pull off onto the shoulder of the road.

3) Safely exit the car and check the hood latch(es). Try closing the hood. If the latch does not lock, secure the hood; do not operate the car until the hood is secure.

4) Hood opening drill:

 NOTE

We suggest you roll down the window before you start so you can hear the person who is in front opening the hood. Make sur when someone is in front of the car (or near the car) that the car is in park with the parking brake on.

a) Go to an empty parking lot. Parent, exit the car and carefully open the hood. Leave the hood up to purposely thwart your teen's visibility.

b) Get back into the car and also have your teen driver roll down their driver side window.

c) Have your teen drive at a speed of 3-5 mph with the hood open while peeking in the crack between the hood and out the driver's side window to simulate the emergency.

✎ NOTE

Even if the teen can see between the crack in front, have the teen stick their head out of the driver's side window to attempt to see the road. Using both viewing options will prepare them best for the actual emergency.

DRILL 2: BRAKES FAIL (PRETEND-PRACTICE DRILL)

Discuss with your teen what they would do in one of the scariest situations imaginable: the brakes fail while they're driving:

1) Immediately lift foot from the gas pedal to slow the car.

2) Remain calm; pump the brakes in an attempt to restore braking.

3) If the car is equipped with an emergency brake—not just a parking brake which will not stop a vehicle—depress the emergency brake pedal or engage the emergency brake lever.

4) Even a parking brake may slow down the car slightly, potentially saving your life.

5) As needed, warn other motorists by using the horn.

6) If the car's brakes are still not working and the emergency brake does not bring the vehicle to a stop here are some unattractive options in order of preference:

    i. pray (just kidding... you can do that later).

    ii. drive up a hill.

---

   iii.   if the shoulder accesses soft dirt, drive onto the shoulder of the road to roll over the dirt to slow the car.

   iv.   drive on an empty field of dirt or grass.

   v.   rub the vehicle's tires against a curb.

   vi.   run the vehicle over shrubbery.

✪ *Life-Saving Tip* ✪

As an absolute last ditch effort to slow down, side swipe as gently as possible vehicles or objects without hitting those objects head on... the more little swipes the better. Sure, insurance rates may go up, but you'll be alive to pay them.

If you have properly maintained the brakes, a brake failure may be the fault of the manufacturer or dealer. Remember, striking a pole or car or any stationary object head-on can be life threatening; the goal is to slow the car by taking several small jolts, rather than a deadly big one. [Note: This is a drill to simulate, rather than actually running into things.]

DRILL 3: FLAT TIRE OR TIRE BLOWOUT (PRETEND-PRACTICE DRILL)

Ask your teen what they would do if they experienced a flat tire or tire blowout or a flat tire while driving. In both cases, it is important to remain calm. Have them practice the following after yelling out 'flat tire' or 'blowout.'

❓ DEFINITION

A flat tire *is a tire whose air pressure is released, and a* tire blowout *is the loss of the rubber portion or tread of the tire.*

Tire Loses Air (Flat Tire)

1) Grasp steering wheel firmly.

2) Do not slam on the brakes.

3) Release the gas pedal and allow the car to slow down before applying the brakes.

4) Steer off the road in a safe and secure place.

5) Make sure the vehicle is out of the way of traffic and on level ground before attempting to change the tire.

---

6) Do not drive on flat tire more than a mile or two or you risk damage to your car.

Tire Blows Out

1) Grasp steering wheel firmly.
2) Take foot off gas—DO NOT step on brakes.
3) Activate flashers.
4) Steer off the road.
5) Apply brakes carefully.
6) Make sure the vehicle is out of the way of traffic and on level ground before attempting to change the tire.

$$$ *Money-Saving Tip* $$$

Never travel more than a mile or you risk ruining your wheels and causing serious damage to your car. This tip alone can save you hundreds, even thousands, of dollars on your repair bill depending on the damage that propagates into your suspension and axles.

⚠ CAUTION!

If a tire goes flat or blows out on the freeway, the driver instantly needs to determine if they can safely exit. If not, they may have to bring the car into the safety lane (if available) on the fast lane of the freeway.

⚠ WARNING!

*Stop the vehicle as soon as possible but **only in a safe place**. In other words, don't have a blowout in the fast lane on the freeway and then stop the vehicle in the fast lane. Drive off the freeway—at 5mph if need be! Ruin your rim. Your life is more valuable than your rim.*

DRILL 4: THE GAS PEDAL STICKS (PRETEND-PRACTICE DRILL)

Ask your teen what they would do if the gas pedal becomes stuck in the 'go' position:

1) Explain, as in all emergencies, they should remain calm and keep both hands on the wheel.

Traffic Safety Consultants, Inc.   *63*

2) With a foot, while looking straight ahead, try to pry the gas pedal back up (while paying attention to the road). If unsuccessful, place the car's transmission lever into neutral (the engine will race and be loud).

3) Brake, and as the car slows, turn the ignition off. (Do not turn the ignition 'all the way off,' but only to the position that disconnects the engine ignition.

4) Steer the car off the paved surface, bringing it to a stop.

5) When stopped, place the car's transmission into 'park.'

6) Open the hood and check the gas pedal's linkage, moving it back and forth. Close the hood and restart the engine. If it still races, shut off the engine and call for assistance.

DRILL 5: VEHICLE COMING HEAD-ON (PRETEND-PRACTICE DRILL)

Ask your teen how they would respond to a vehicle coming at them in their lane of travel at high speed—the scariest incident on the road.

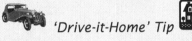

'Drive-it-Home' Tip

Head-on collisions are the most dangerous type of collision and every attempt should be made to avoid them.

If a car is coming at you:

1) Place both hands on the steering wheel, and carefully, rapidly slow your car. [Reducing the combined speed of colliding vehicles reduces the damage of the collision.]

2) Flash the car's headlights and honk the horn.

3) Assess the situation quickly to determine how to avoid the oncoming car. Almost always steer right, not left.

4) Steer off the paved potion of the road if necessary.

5) It may be necessary to hit a fixed object, or series of fixed objects, off the roadway, which is far preferable to striking the other car head-on. [Fixed objects have no speed or kinetic energy whereas the oncoming vehicle has very high energy. It is best to hit softer objects such as branches or shrubbery rather than concrete or trees.]

6) When steering back onto the road, do so gradually.

Fast reactions, staying calm, being wholly aware of imminent objects and people, and sensible decision-making are the keys to surviving this terrifying emergency condition. Most important, remind your teen to always look ahead and identify potential emergencies long before they happen. Safe, defensive driving is the word.

CULMINATION DRILL

In this culmination drill your teen performs all the driving drills in succession to demonstrate mastery. For emergency drills, the drills are rehearsal only.

 Now enjoy the well-deserved 'Ice Cream Drill,' as described for Lesson 1 (page 23). Savor the moment. Congratulations, you have successfully drilled for emergencies! Well done!

Summary of Lesson

In this final lesson, your teen learns to handle emergencies by staying calm. The more you continue to simulate and practice these emergency techniques, the better your teen will be prepared for the real thing.

 LIGHTER TURN

The best substitute for experience is being sixteen.
— *Raymond Duncan*

Parental Tips For Reducing Teen Collisions

Teenage drivers are ranked as some of the most dangerous drivers. Lack of driving experience is one of the main reasons. Another reason is a *reduced sense of fear*. Compared with older drivers, teenagers as a group are more willing to take risks and less likely to use safety belts. They also are more likely than older drivers to underestimate the dangers associated with hazardous situations and less able to cope with such dangers.

The cause of many teenage crashes is not an issue of insufficient skills or knowledge. It's often an issue of attitude and maturity. There is no magical solution in preventing teenage crashes. This guidebook and its many tips is only as a way to assist you as a parent in helping your teenage driver to be a safe and responsible motor vehicle operator and maybe just save their life!

Conclusion

On behalf of Traffic Safety Consultants, Inc., it has been an honor to work with you and your teen on our driving course. Our journey took us through the basics of starting a car to 'driving like a star' at nighttime. We took some twists and turns and drove the faster streets of our neighborhoods, while carefully navigating dangerous intersections. We tried to have fun with the course without ever sugar coating the safety.

We know this educational journey is just the beginning and suggest you always continue to learn about cars and traffic safety—to become an even better and more defensive driver. For more information please go to our Website www.TeenDrivingOnline.com and, especially, consult the online addendum to this guidebook: *Teach Your Teen, Plus*.

As a Safe Driving Samaritan and esteemed graduate of *Teach Your Teen To Drive and Stay Alive*, we ask one simple favor: always pass along the government crash Website of www.safercars.gov to anyone considering buying a car—new or used: the car they drive can save their lives.

And if you enjoyed our course, the greatest compliment we can receive is if you recommend this book to a friend. Thank you for taking the journey and for sharing our passion for safety behind the wheel. Please be cautious, careful, and courteous.

Sincerely,

Brett and Bruce Elkins

Congratulations:

... for graduating from the Teach Your Teen to Drive and Stay Alive Course. You have demonstrated a mastery of safe driving techniques and the understanding of the importance of the ice cream culmination drill. May all of your driving experience be safe and this sweet!

About the Authors

Bruce Elkins—(master's degree in public health and safety, California State University, Los Angeles; bachelor of science, University of Southern California (USC)): Mr. Elkins is known nationwide as the father/creator of Comedy Traffic Schools, having taught traffic safety for more than 45 years with a creative flair and an infectious personality. In 1978, Mr. Elkins was awarded a two year grant by the Office of Traffic Safety (OTS) to implement bicycle and moped safety programs in the Los Angeles Unified School District (LAUSD). He helped create the initial curriculum for the LAUSD's juvenile and adult program where he also taught history, driver's education and training, as an area supervisor. Mr. Elkins is currently president of Cheap School, one of the nation's leading traffic schools; he has graduated more than two million students as an operator of traffic safety programs nationwide. Mr. Elkins has also served as the vice president and/or secretary of several traffic safety organizations, including the California Traffic School Association (CTSA). His passion is USC football and his family. He has two children: an ophthalmologist in Los Angeles and Brett Elkins, with whom he authored the book.

Brett Elkins—(bachelor of science, USC Magna Cum Laude School). Brett is the president and CEO of Traffic Safety Consultants (TSC), Inc. The company, also known as Comedy School, is the nation's largest traffic school organization having graduated 2.5 million students since 1976, operating in 200 cities with several hundred affiliates nationwide. Mr. Elkins is the past executive vice president of the CTSA. His passion is racquetball where he serves on several boards, esp. Chairman of the World Outdoor Racquetball Hall of Fame (WORHOF). He is president and cofounder of www.SportsChampionship.com an innovative Website that enables people to connect and play anyone anywhere 24-7. Brett is married with four children and lives in Los Angeles. His father, coauthor Bruce Elkins, taught Brett how to drive (and stay alive) when Brett was a teen.

Made in the USA
San Bernardino, CA
02 September 2019